The Bush T[...]
and Drum Theatr[...]
present the world

C000103348

Airsick

by Emma Frost

8 October - 8 November 2003 at The Bush Theatre, London
13 - 29 November 2003 at The Drum Theatre Plymouth

Directed by Mike Bradwell
Designed by Es Devlin
Lighting by Jason Taylor
Sound design by Nick Manning

thebushtheatre

Cast (In order of appearance)

Lucy	Celia Robertson
Mick	Peter Jonfield
Gabriel	Gideon Turner
Scarlet	Susannah Doyle
Joe	Eric Loren

Credits

Director	Mike Bradwell
Set & Costume Designer	Es Devlin
Lighting Designer	Jason Taylor
Associate Lighting Designer	Matt Kirby
Sound Designer	Nick Manning
Assistant Director	Lucy Foster
Deputy Stage Manager	Georgie Gunn
Costume Supervisor / Assistant Stage Manager	Penny Challen
Wall and Ceiling Construction	Theatre Royal Plymouth TR2
Floor Construction	Andy Beauchamp
Additional Construction	Rajesh Westerburg
Painting	Richard Nutbourne
Press Representation	The Sarah Mitchell Partnership 020 7434 1944
Graphic Design	Emma Cooke
	emma@chamberlainmcauley.co.uk

This performance lasts approximately 2 hours plus interval.
The play was commissioned by The Bush Theatre with the support of The
Peggy Ramsay Foundation Project Award 2002 and received it's first performance on
Wednesday 8th October 2003 at The Bush Theatre, London.

The Bush Theatre would like to offer special thanks to Sue Mercer at Sainsburys,
Daniel Todd at Alba, The Royal Opera House and The Royal National Theatre.

At The Bush Theatre

Artistic Director	Mike Bradwell
Executive Producer	Fiona Clark
General Manager	Brenda Newman
Literary Manager	Nicola Wilson
Head of Marketing	Sam McAuley for Chamberlain McAuley
Marketing Officer	Gillian Jones
Development Manager	Nicky Jones
Production Manager	Pam Vision
Chief Electrician	Matt Kirby
Resident Stage Manager	Ros Terry
Assistant General Manager	Alex Mercer
Literary Assistant	Frances Stirk
Box Office Supervisor	Dominique Gerrard
Box Office Assistants	Rowan Bangs
	Michael Wagg
Front of House Duty Managers	Kellie Batchelor
	Caroline Beckman
	Johnny Flynn
	Vanessa Lucas-Smith
	Sarah O'Neill
	Rebecca Wolsey
Associate Artists	Tanya Burns
	Es Devlin
*Pearson Writer in Residence	Simon Burt
Sheila Lemon Writer in Residence	Chloe Moss

*The Bush Theatre has the support of the Pearson Playwrights' Scheme sponsored by the Olivier Foundation

The Bush Theatre is the winner of The Peggy Ramsay Foundation Project Award 2002

The Alternative Theatre Company Ltd (The Bush Theatre)
Shepherds Bush Green, London W12 8QD

www.bushtheatre.co.uk
email:info@bushtheatre.co.uk
Box Office: 020 7610 4224
Administration: 020 7602 3703

Registered company no 1221968
Registered charity no 270080.
Vat no 288316873

Cast

Susannah Doyle (Scarlet)

Theatre credits include *Death of Cool* (Hampstead), *Love You Too* (The Bush Theatre), *Hurly Burly* (Old Vic/West End), *Looking at You Revived / Again* (The Bush Theatre/Leicester Haymarket), *Man and Superman* (Glasgow Citizens), *View From A Bridge* (Sheffield Crucible) and *Oedipus Flabbergasted* (Cochrane Theatre).

Television credits include *Midsomer Murders* (ITV), *Cold Feet* (Granada), *As If* (Carnival Films), *Ballykissangel* (BBC), *Drop The Dead Donkey* (Hat Trick), *A Touch of Frost* (Yorkshire TV), *Hospital* (Tiger Aspect), *Soldier Soldier* (Central), *Dirty Something* (BBC Screen Two), *Work* (Channel 4) and *Young Indiana Jones* (Lucas Films).

Film credits include *About A Boy* (Working Title), *The Lovers* (Saltire Film & TV), *Don't Go Breaking My Heart* (Kenright Films), *Another Man Another Woman* (Power Pictures), *His 'n' Hers* (Fifth Floor Films) and *Scandal* (Scala Films).

Peter Jonfield (Mick)

Theatre credits include *All My Sons* (Northcott Theatre), *Moonshine* (Hampstead/Plymouth), *Shang-a-Lang* (The Bush Theatre), *Loot* (Plymouth Theatre Royal), *Plunder* (No 1 Tour & West End), *Four Door Saloon* (Hampstead Theatre Club), *Scenes From an Execution* (Almeida Theatre), and *The Resistable Rise of Artuo Ui* (Borderline Theatre Company), as well as two-and-a-half-years with Pip Simmons Theatre Group and seasons at Glasgow Citizens Theatre, Liverpool Playhouse, Oxford Playhouse and the Young Vic.

Television credits include *Silent Witness* (BBC), *Smith & Jones* (1997/8, Talkback), *The Famous Five Series 2* (Zenith North), *Bramwell* (Whitby Davidson), *Sharpe's Regiment* (ITV), *Spender* (BBC), *Sherlock Holmes* (Granada), *Blooming Youth* (BBC) and *Wilderness Road* (BBC).

Film credits include *Frankenstein*, *Age of Treason*, *Let Him Have It*, *A Fish Called Wanda*, *Murder by Decree*, *McVicar*, *The Time Bandits*, *Rememberance*, Pink Floyd's *The Wall*, *Clockwise* and *Bellman and True*.

Cast

Eric Loren (Joe)

Theatre credits include *The Boy Who Fell Into a Book* (English Touring), *Stop Kiss* (Soho Theatre), *The Maiden's Prayer* (The Bush), *All My Sons* (Theatre Royal, Plymouth), *Company* (Library Theatre), *A Lie of The Mind* (Battersea Arts Centre), *Disappeared* (Leicester Haymarket/Tour/Royal Court), *Beau Jest* (Birmingham Stage Co./Tour/Bloomsbury Theatre), *Someone Who'll Watch Over Me* (Gateway, Chester), *Broadway Bound* (The Library, Manchester), *Brighton Beach Memoirs* (Salisbury Playhouse), *Little Shop of Horrors* and *The Iceman Cometh* (Lyric Theatre Belfast) and *Guys and Dolls* (Cheltenham Everyman).

Television credits include *Great Industrial Wonders* (BBC), *Wyrdsister* (Granada), *Big Bad World* (Carlton), *Over Here* (BBC), *Unnatural Pursuits* (BBC), *Flight Terminal* (Granada) and *Medics* (Granada).

Film credits include *Never Say Never Mind* (Revenge Films), *The Labyrinth* (Lupo Productions), *Saving Private Ryan* (DW Productions), *The Scorsese Way* (Channel 4), *The Saint* (Paramount Pictures), *Hackers* (United Artists), *Memphis Belle* (Enigma Films) and *Night Breed* (Sparkline Ltd).

Celia Robertson (Lucy)

Theatre credits include *Swimming in The Shallows* (Hen & Chickens and Pleasance, Edinburgh), *Handbag* (A.T.C at Lyric Studio and UK Tour), *Love and Understanding* (Bush and Long Wharf, USA), *What do I Get?* (Old Red Lion), *The Maids* (Shoreditch Studio) and *A Week With Tony* (Finborough).

Television credits include *Bad Girls* and *The Blooding*.

Gideon Turner (Gabriel)

Theatre credits include *Modern Man* (New End Theatre), *Richard III* (Sheffield Crucible), *Don Juan* (Sheffield Crucible), *A Midsummer Night's Dream* and *Love's Labour Lost* (The Open Air Theatre, Regents Park), *Edward II* (Sheffield Crucible), *Ghost Stories* (St Mary's, Brighton), *The Death of Cool* (Hampstead), *Heritage* (Hampstead), *The Pitchford Disney* (Bolton Octagon) and *Arcadia* (RNT Tour).

Television credits include *Cromwell* (BBC), *Boudica* (Box Films), *Starhunter* (USA and Canada), *Cinderella* (Channel 4), *Dark Realm* (Warner Brothers), *Bad Girls* (Shed Productions), *Dalziel and Pascoe IV* (BBC), *Dangerfield* (BBC), *The Stalker's Apprentice* (Scottish TV), *David* (TNT), *Heartbeat* (Yorkshire TV) and *Casualty* (BBC).

Film credits include *Loop* and *Poppy's Present* (Picture That Productions).

Other work includes a music video for The Darkness (MTV) and *Smelling of Roses* (BBC Radio 4).

Creative Team

Emma Frost Writer

Airsick is Emma's first stage play and was commissioned with a Bush Theatre / Peggy Ramsay Project Award bursary.

Film credits include: *The Fall* (1998); *One Moment* (Shooting 2003); *Agnes* (in development). Emma also writes for television.

Emma worked as a script editor and Head of Development for several film and TV companies before moving into writing.

Mike Bradwell Director

Mike trained at E15 Acting School. He played Norman in Mike Leigh's award winning film *Bleak Moments*, was an actor/musician with The Ken Campbell Road Show and an Underwater Escapologist with Hirst's Carivari. He founded Hull Truck theatre company in 1971 and directed all their shows for 10 years including his own plays *Oh What*, *Bridget's House*, *Bed of Roses*, *Ooh La La!*, *Still Crazy After All These Years* and new plays by Doug Lucie, Alan Williams and Peter Tinniswood. Mike has directed 33 shows at The Bush, including *Hard Feelings* by Doug Lucie; *Unsuitable for Adults* by Terry Johnson, *The Fosdyke Sagas* by Bill Tidy and Alan Plater; *Love and Understanding* by Joe Penhall (also at The Long Wharf Theatre, U.S.A); *Love You, Too* by Doug Lucie; *Dead Sheep* and *Shang-a-Lang* by Catherine Johnson (also 1999 national tour); *Howie The Rookie* by Mark O'Rowe (also Civic Theatre, Tallaght and Andrew's Lane theatres, Dublin, 1999 Edinburgh Festival, Plymouth Theatre Royal, the Tron, Glasgow, PS122 New York and the Magic Theatre, San Francisco); *Dogs Barking* by Richard Zajdllic, *Normal* by Helen Blakeman, *Resident Alien* by Tim Fountain (also for New York Theater Workshop), *Flamingos* by Jonathan Hall, *Blackbird* by Adam Rapp, *The Glee Club* by Richard Cameron and *Little Baby Nothing* by Catherine Johnson. He has also directed new plays by Helen Cooper, G.F Newman, Jonathan Gems, Richard Cameron, Flann O'Brien and Terry Johnson at Hampstead Theatre, the Tricycle, King's Head, West Yorkshire Playhouse, Science Fiction Theatre of Liverpool, The National Theatre of Brent, The Rude Players of Winnipeg and The Royal Court, where he was Associate Director. Mike has written and directed for television including *The Writing on the Wall*; *Games Without Frontiers*; *Chains of Love* and *Happy Feet* (BBC Screen One). Mike is Artistic Director of The Bush Theatre.

Lucy Foster Assistant Director

Lucy has recently graduated from Oxford University, where she was President of Oxford University Drama Society. While there she directed new writing, the devised piece *Crossed Wire*, and Sarah Kane's *Crave*, which was selected for the 2002 National Student Drama Festival. *Crave* won a Judge's Individual Award and the assistant directing placement at The Bush. Since graduating, Lucy has assisted on a scratch performance of *Newsnight the Opera* at Battersea Arts Centre and worked with Mike Bradwell on *Nine Parts of Desire* at The Bush.

Creative Team

Es Devlin Designer

Es has been associate artist at The Bush Theatre since 1997. Over the course of 4 productions with Mike Bradwell she developed an approach to the theatre's 45 cubic metres of space which culminated in the three pierced glowing planes of *Howie the Rookie* – which won TMA Best Design 1999.

Subsequently her collaborators have included the post/pre-punk band WIRE and Jake and Dinos Chapman at the Barbican, Eddie Izzard on Broadway, The Pet Shop Boys at the Arts and a range of choreographers, directors and writers at Rambert Dance Co, Out of Joint, the RSC and RNT. Es's most recent project was a giant conjuror's transformation box for *Macbeth*, Klangbogen Festival Vienna.

She is currently designing *Five Gold Rings* for the Almeida (opens December 18th), *The Spanish Golden Age Season* at the RSC Swan (Spring 2004) and *Wagner's Ring Cycle* for the Royal Opera House in collaboration with the architect Daniel Libeskind (December 2004 - October 2006). Es's work can be viewed at www.esdevlin.com.

Jason Taylor Lighting Designer

Recent and current work includes *Madness of King George 3rd* (West Yorkshire Playhouse), *Us and Them* (Hampstead Theatre), *Hobson's Choice* and *Yerma* (Royal Exchange Theatre), *The Green Man* (Theatre Royal Plymouth/The Bush Theatre), *Abigails Party* (New Ambassadors/Whitehall/National Tour), *Pretending To Be Me* (Comedy Theatre), *Little Shop of Horrors* (West Yorkshire Playhouse), *My Night With Reg/Dealers Choice* (Birmingham Rep), *The Clearing* (Shared Experience), *Single Spies* (National Tour), *Sitting Pretty* (National Tour), *Pirates of Penzance* (National Tour), *Office* (Edinburgh International Festival), *Hedda Gabler* and *Snake in The Fridge* (Royal Exchange Theatre), *The Dead Eye Boy* (Hampstead Theatre) and *Lolanthe*, *The Mikado* and *Yeoman of The Guard* (Savoy Theatre).

Jason has lit over 200 other productions including 14 seasons at the Open Air Theatre, *Kindertransport* (Vaudeville), *Rosencrantz* and *Guildenstern* (Piccadilly Theatre), *And Then There Were None* (Duke of York's Theatre) and *Great Balls of Fire* (Cambridge Theatre). Other London work includes productions at The Bush, Hampstead, The Bridewell and numerous productions for Soho Theatre. He is also lighting consultant for the new Soho Theatre and the Open Air Theatre, Regents Park.

Nick Manning Sound Designer

Nick Trained in stage management at The Central School of Speech and Drama and is currently working as The Lyric Hammersmith's Sound Technician. Recent work includes *Rabbit* (Frantic Assembly), *Great Expectations* (Bristol Old Vic), *Pericles*, *Camille*, *A Christmas Carol*, *The Prince of Homburg*, *Aladdin*, *The Servant*, *Pinocchio* and *The White Devil* (Lyric), *Out of Our Heads – Susan & Janice* (ATC & Edinburgh Fringe). Previously he worked at Derby Playhouse and the Gordon Craig Theatre where productions include *Cinderella*, *The Wizard of Oz* and *Godspell*.

Matt Kirby Associate Lighting Designer

Matt has been Chief Electrician at The Bush Theatre since 2001. Recent design credits include *Sakina's Restaurant*, *The Age of Consent*, and the London re-light for *Nine Parts of Desire* at The Bush Theatre. Other projects include *Pale Horse* and *Blue Remembered Hills* for Five Go Theatre Co, and various projects for Birmingham School of Speech and Drama.

The Bush Theatre

The Bush Theatre opened in April 1972 in the upstairs dining room of The Bush Hotel, Shepherds Bush Green. The room had previously served as Lionel Blair's dance studio. Since then, The Bush has become the country's leading new writing venue with over 350 productions, premiering the finest new writing talent.

"One of the most vibrant theatres in Britain, and a consistent hotbed of new writing talent." Midweek magazine

Playwrights whose works have been performed here at The Bush include: Stephen Poliakoff, Robert Holman, Tina Brown, Snoo Wilson, John Byrne, Ron Hutchinson, Terry Johnson, Beth Henley, Kevin Elyot, Doug Lucie, Dusty Hughes, Sharman Macdonald, Billy Roche, Tony Kushner, Catherine Johnson, Philip Ridley, Richard Cameron, Jonathan Harvey, Richard Zajdlic, Naomi Wallace, David Eldridge, Conor McPherson, Joe Penhall, Helen Blakeman, Lucy Gannon, Mark O'Rowe and Charlotte Jones.

The theatre has also attracted major acting and directing talents including Bob Hoskins, Alan Rickman, Antony Sher, Stephen Rea, Frances Barber, Lindsay Duncan, Brian Cox, Kate Beckinsale, Patricia Hodge, Simon Callow, Alison Steadman, Jim Broadbent, Tim Roth, Jane Horrocks, Gwen Taylor, Mike Leigh, Mike Figgis, Mike Newell and Richard Wilson.

Victoria Wood and Julie Walters first worked together at The Bush, and Victoria wrote her first sketch on an old typewriter she found backstage.

In over 30 years, The Bush has won more than one hundred awards and recently received The Peggy Ramsay Foundation Project Award 2002. Bush plays, including most recently *The Glee Club*, have transferred to the West End. Off-Broadway transfers include *Howie the Rookie* and *Resident Alien*. Film adaptations include *Beautiful Thing* and *Disco Pigs*. Bush productions have toured throughout Britain, Europe and North America, most recently *Stitching*. *Adrenalin... Heart* will transfer to the Tokyo International Festival in 2004.

Every year we receive over fifteen hundred scripts through the post, and we read them all. According to The Sunday Times:

"What happens at The Bush today is at the very heart of tomorrow's theatre"

That's why we read all the scripts we receive and will continue to do so.

Mike Bradwell
Artistic Director

Fiona Clark
Executive Producer

Support The Bush – Patron Scheme

Be There At The Beginning

The Bush Theatre is a writer's theatre – dedicated to commissioning, developing and producing exclusively new plays. Up to seven writers each year are commissioned and we offer a bespoke programme of workshops and one-to-one dramaturgy to develop their plays. Our international reputation of over thirty years is built on consistently producing the very best work to the very highest standard.

With your help this work can continue to flourish.

The Bush Theatre's Patron Scheme delivers an exciting range of opportunities for individual and corporate giving, offering a closer relationship with the theatre and a wide range of benefits from ticket offers to special events. Above all, it is an ideal way to acknowledge your support for one of the world's greatest new writing theatres.

To join, please pick up an information pack from the foyer, call Nicky Jones, Development Manager on 020 7602 3703 or email development@bushtheatre.co.uk

We would like to thank our current members and invite you to join them!

Rookies
Anonymous
Anonymous
Anonymous
Brian Cox
Susan Davenport
David Day
Leslie Forbes, Author
Lucy Heller
Mr G Hopkinson
Ian Metherell
Ray Miles
Malcolm & Liliane Ogden
Paul L Oppenheimer
Clare Rich & Robert Marshall
Edward Smith
Toby Young

Beautiful Things
Anonymous
Mr and Mrs Simon Bass
Alan Brodie
Clive Butler
Clyde Cooper
Patrick and Anne Foster
Albert Fuss
Vivien Goodwin
Ken Griffin
Sheila Hancock
David Hare
Philip Jackson
William Keeling
Adam Kenwright
The Mackintosh Foundation
Laurie Marsh
John Reynolds
Mr and Mrs George Robinson
Tracey Scoffield
Barry Serjent
Brian D Smith
Samuel West
Richard Zajdlic

Glee Club
Anonymous
The Hon Mrs Giancarla Alen-Buckley
Jim Broadbent
Alan Rickman
Annette Stone

Lone Star
Princess of Darkness

Bronze Corporate Membership
Act Productions Ltd
Oberon Books Ltd
Working Title Film/WT2

Silver Corporate Membership
The Agency

Platinum Corporate Membership
Anonymous

Drum Theatre Plymouth 2003

For the past five years, the Drum Theatre Plymouth has become a theatre of origination, producing new writing, physical theatre and other innovative work for Plymouth and the South West. As part of the Theatre Royal Plymouth complex, it has become a leading force in the national development of writing, directing and producing relationships.

Recent premieres have included *Edward Gant's Amazing Feats of Loneliness* by Anthony Neilson, *The Green Man* by Doug Lucie, subsequently produced at the Bush Theatre, *Doorman/Bouncer* with Crewes Gale Productions and *Mr Placebo* by Isabel Wright in a collaboration with the Traverse Theatre, Edinburgh.

In addition to *Airsick*, our current autumn programme includes *Rabbit* by Brendan Cowell, a co-production with our long-term associates Frantic Assembly, and Gregory Burke's highly acclaimed *The Straits* in a co-production with Paines Plough and Hampstead Theatre.

We also present the latest works from Graeae, Told By An Idiot and The Royal Court, The Red Room and Out of Joint, as well as a popular, annual Christmas residency from Pop Up.

Simon Stokes
Artistic Director

www.theatreroyal.com

Chief Executive	Adrian Vinken
Artistic Director	Simon Stokes
General Manager	Alan Finch
Technical Director	Ed Wilson

TR2 | The Production & Education Centre

As part of its 21st Birthday celebrations in 2003, the Theatre Royal opened TR2 – Europe's first purpose-built Production & Education Centre in Plymouth. This state of the art building provides unrivalled production, wardrobe and rehearsal facilities, as well as becoming a cultural resource for the people of the South West. TR2 has now won two of the major annual architectural prizes in Britain, the Design Excellence Award from the American Institute of Architects, and also the Building of the Year from the Royal Fine Art Commission.

The Theatre Royal's Education Team provides an essential resource for developing audiences and participation by running two youth and community theatres. It also works with schools throughout the South West in the form of skills-based workshops and large scale performance projects. In addition to this the Education Team exclusively train local practitioners and young company members in the technique of workshops, providing the region with a highly skilled base of resources, and are also proud to be the regional centre for National Connections Festival in the South West.

TR2 | The Details

- TR2 was conceived to meet both the particularly high production workload that Plymouth supports, as well as the needs of its extensive education programme.
- Our 500 strong Young Company bases all its activities in the building as does our large People's Company for older groups.
- The site had to be created from a tidal mud flat by excavating a nearby quarry and transporting crushed limestone to the site to reclaim six acres from the water.
- TR2's landlord is the Duchy of Cornwall.
- The Theatre's joiners, metal fabricators, prop makers, wardrobe staff and scenic artists will occupy a range of spacious and bright workshop spaces.
- Glowing woven bronze material clads rehearsal rooms and education workshops and walls of beaten zinc and glass look over the rock landscape dropping down to the edge of the River Plym.
- TR2 has already been earmarked as a future national training centre for specialist craft based theatre-making skills.
- Visitors can view a new show is coming together in Wardrobe, Props and Construction from glazed gantries above the departments.
- The first show to be built at TR2 was *Cats* for the current tour, closely followed by *Jus' Like That*, directed by Simon Callow, *Summer Holiday* for its National Tour and *Blown* by Nicholas Field. In this autumn season TR2 is building *Scrooge* and *The Taming Of The Shrew*, both of which will tour No. 1 theatre's nationally following their runs in Plymouth.

AIRSICK

Emma Frost

For T

Thanks to

Ligeia Marsh.
Nikki Grier, James Tovell, Andrew Neil,
Rosamund Barker, Rob Messik and Angela McSherry
for being there at the beginning.

Tanya Vickers, Ronaldo Vasconcellos, Jo Smith,
Angie Brooker and Janine Gray
for huge support.

And big, big thanks to Mike Bradwell, Fiona Clark,
Nicola Wilson, Simon Stokes and all at
the Bush Theatre and Drum Theatre, Plymouth.

2

Characters

LUCY, *early thirties*
SCARLET, *early thirties*
MICK, *sixty-ish, Lucy's father*
GABRIEL, *late-twenties New Zealander*
JOE, *mid-thirties East Coast American*

The two *men* in Scene One could be played by stage crew,
or failing that, by the actors playing Gabriel and Joe

The *woman* in the final scene should not be played by actresses
playing Lucy or Scarlet

A stroke (/) marks the point of interruption in overlapping
dialogue

*The action takes place in East London between June and
October 2002*

Scene One.

A black hole spins and sucks silently in space. From the darkness, a voice:

LUCY. On 4th October 1968, American scientist John Wheeler named Black Holes. It was morning in Princeton and he'd just finished eating his egg. He peered into the shell, at the yellow remains – and it came to him. The most destructive force in the universe: 'Black Holes'. The French weren't too happy. Their translation, 'trou noir', implied something rather dodgy about female parts so the journals wouldn't print it because they thought it was obscene –

Lights up on LUCY, *self conscious in a white hospital gown, as she stands before the black hole.*

Sorry I'm ranting . . . It's just . . . I know this because the 4th of October 1968 is also the day I was born. It wasn't particularly remarkable, a dreary day my mum said, but the usual well-wishers came, predicted health, wealth and happiness. They said I'd be a star. (*Beat.*) My mum said I used to suck the mud off stones, I don't remember.

My first memory is of my fifth birthday party . . .

The sound of a children's party fades in and three men enter, one of whom is LUCY*'s father,* MICK. *He is dressed in black, with a heavy black overcoat. One of the other men holds a yellow plastic tray, the other a hard backed book.*

We were running round the house trying to catch Scarlet, my best friend, who was acting weird . . . when my *dad* appeared. Usually he stayed as far away from children as he could, a dark presence behind a closed door, so it was strange to see him knee deep in streamers, forcing on a smile. He told us we were going to play a game. And all I could think was that if *my dad* had come to my party, if my dad was going to play a game with us, then I, Lucy, would be first.

MICK. Here you go then, put this on.

MICK *ties a blindfold round* LUCY*'s eyes. The other men put the tray on the floor and move her forward onto it.*

Right. You're going on a journey, and it's a long way from here so you've gotta go by plane.

The roar of plane engines, rising.

LUCY. I hear the engines roar, a tightness in my throat. I buckle my seatbelt round me.

MICK. But the only trouble is, the plane's held together with Sellotape and string, 'cause it's so old!

SECOND MAN. Cabin crew, ready for take off.

LUCY. Sellotape and string . . .

The engines are really roaring now. MICK *and one of the men take hold of the tray.*

MICK. Sellotape and string and rubber bands. But there's no other way to get there and you've gotta go / so you've got no choice . . .

LUCY. My heart is beating. I feel myself lift / off.

MICK *and the other man inch the tray off the ground.*

MICK. And she's up. Into the air, higher and / higher.

LUCY. A sudden lurch. I hold on tight. I've lost all sense of time and space . . .

The tray now weaves high and round and about, disorientating LUCY.

MICK. Way up above the ground. We're over London, over all the little / houses.

LUCY. I'm frightened, head spinning. But I don't let on.

MICK. Ah! Oh no! But the rubber bands are snapping! The plane is breaking up!

LUCY. No! / NO!

They start to wobble the tray, which is now only two inches above the ground, but LUCY *in her blindfold has lost all sense of space and doesn't know this.*

MEN. Oh no, Lucy! She's breaking up! She's breaking up! But you're too high! You're on the / ceiling!

As he speaks the second man holds the hard-backed book on top of LUCY*'s head so that it feels like the ceiling.*

LUCY. I feel the ceiling above my head.

MICK. The rubber bands are going! The wings are falling off!

LUCY. No! Daddy! No!

MICK. You're on the ceiling! But you're gonna have to jump!

LUCY. I'm too high!

MEN (*wobbling the tray around*). She's breaking up, Lucy!

MICK. Lucy! You gotta JUMP! Take a big jump Lucy!

The sound of the engines plummeting towards the ground.

MICK / MEN. Jump! Lucy, / jump!

LUCY. No!

MICK. JUMP! JUMP!

Almost sobbing, LUCY *takes a huge breath.*

She leaps into the void.

Blackout. The sound of children laughing gradually fading.

The distant sound of a plane landing.

Scene Two.

Heathrow Airport arrivals hall.

A sense of bustle. Announcements over speakers about flight arrivals from the US.

LUCY *walks unsteadily through, obviously feeling sick. She takes her large suitcase from the carousel, then vomits on the floor.*

A passing man, GABRIEL, *easy charm, infectious, watches her. He comes over.*

GABRIEL. Are you . . . alright? (*Beat.*) Is there anything . . . ?

LUCY *shakes her head.*

Do you want some water?

She looks up as he offers a bottle of water out, and fishes for a tissue. She takes them.

LUCY. Thanks. Sorry.

He shakes his head, it's OK.

GABRIEL. Come here, let them clean it up. Sit down for a minute.

He steers her away. LUCY *sits down on her upended suitcase.*

LUCY. Sorry, it's just . . . *flying*. I thought I was gonna be alright. I wasn't even gonna have a drink because I've just spent most of the last year in New York trying to kill myself with alcohol, but then the film came on, and I couldn't work out why I was getting so stressed – and not just me, everyone – and then I realised, the film's *Chicken Run*, and it's about a bunch of creatures being force fed in a tiny space, and they're all gonna die because they can't fly!

So I lost it. Downed eighteen vodkas and tried for liver damage.

GABRIEL. Quality illness.

LUCY (*smiles*). I suppose you're one of those people who loves flying and is on and off like there's no tomorrow.

GABRIEL *looks like he's about to say no, but then he smiles and nods.*

GABRIEL. If you're going down, you're going down, there's nothing you can do about it. Even the brace position's a load of rubbish. A friend of mine who's a pilot told me. They only tell you to do it so you make less mess. You're still dead, but at least they can find all the pieces.

Sorry, you probably didn't want to know that, did you? Still, look on the bright side. At least they didn't lose your luggage.

LUCY. They lost your luggage?

GABRIEL (*nods*). All I've got is this . . .

He indicates his clothes.

. . . and a 'British-Airways-Lost-My-Luggage-and-All-I-Got-Was-This-Lousy-T-Shirt' T-shirt.

LUCY. They don't really give you one of those, do they?

GABRIEL. No. 'Course not. It just says 'British Airways'. You have to write the rest on yourself. Trouble is, my pen's in the suitcase. Along with the details of the hotel I'm meant to be staying in . . .

LUCY. So what will you do?

GABRIEL. Stay at your house?

LUCY *stiffens, suddenly worried by him.*

S'alright. I'm only joking. You think I'm coming on to you now, don't you?

LUCY. No, 'course not.

Beat.

GABRIEL. I was actually.

I've freaked you out now, haven't I?

LUCY. No, I . . . It's just . . . I've got a boyfriend.

GABRIEL. Yeah, I know. Well, you would. Most people do. But other than that, you'd be interested, would you?

Sorry, it's just . . . why do people say it like that? You know, 'I've got a *boyfriend*', like, 'I've got a gun! So don't come near me or I'll shoot! I'll blow your fucking head off!' You know, 'I've got a boyfriend', like, it's a *bad* thing. Like it's a *permanent* thing, for one thing. Like it's a disease. You know, these things can *change*. They should be a constantly re-assessed bid, not a permanent fixture.

LUCY. So have you got a girlfriend?

GABRIEL. Yeah.

I did have. Before I came away. But . . .

LUCY. It didn't work out?

GABRIEL *sighs, searching for words, then gives in, and, with difficulty –*

GABRIEL. She said I made her sick.

LUCY. I shouldn't think she was perfect either. Anyway, according to my dad, we're all better off on our own anyway.

GABRIEL. Well that's not right, is it?

LUCY. No. I don't know. I suppose not . . .

GABRIEL. Yeah, well . . . I'm just not very good at girlfriends. I always fuck 'em up somehow. Always seem to go out with women who I don't like, or who don't like me, or who are just . . .

LUCY. For what it's worth, I'm not much good either. Show me a man with a serious psychosis and I'm the one he's sleeping with.

GABRIEL. Yeah? So what's your boyfriend's name? Charles Manson?

LUCY. Joe. And he's the exception. Don't know quite how
    I managed it.

GABRIEL. He coming to meet you?

LUCY. No. He's in New York.

GABRIEL. He's American?

She nods.

Work in a tall glass building? Only joking. Still . . .

Optimistic it could go wrong.

. . . long distance relationship . . .

LUCY. He's moving over.

GABRIEL. He's moving over. 'Course he is. I fold.

LUCY. So . . . how long are you staying? In London?

GABRIEL. Till the next flight at this rate.

LUCY (*smiles*). No, but really?

GABRIEL. Dunno. Couple of months maybe. The summer?

LUCY. Look I can't promise anything but . . . I might know
    someone who's got a room to rent? And there's a cheap
    B&B near me I could maybe show you for the meantime . . . ?

GABRIEL. Yeah? Great! If you don't mind.

LUCY. Well, you did look after me. You must be the only man
    in London who doesn't run a mile at the first sign of vomit.

GABRIEL. That's how I like 'em.

She smiles. He holds out his hand.

I'm Gabriel.

LUCY. Lucy.

They shake hands. He picks up her bag as she stands.

GABRIEL. So, what do you do with yourself in London then,
    Lucy?

LUCY (*awkward*). I'm . . . er . . . I'm a *maker*.

I don't like the word 'artist'. It sounds . . . too important.
I think that if you want to make art, you have to remove the
ego. You have to rub yourself out.

He doesn't entirely understand. But he grins.

GABRIEL. So go on then, 'Lucy the artist', what's your favourite colour?

LUCY (*laughs*). My favourite colour? (*He nods.*) Yellow.

Scene Three

LUCY*'s living room.*

MICK, *a dark, heavy presence, sits in a big, black swivel chair, resentfully channel flicking the TV, while* LUCY*'s best friend and flatmate,* SCARLET, *tall, different, unintentionally sexual, busies around collecting a bizarre collection of possessions together.*

MICK *flicks the channel back to EastEnders and sighs annoyance.*

MICK. See this? I don't wanna watch this, do I? Women getting their faces punched! What's that about?!

He makes a dismissive gesture and laughs in disbelief.

Load of bloody rubbish, isn't it?

SCARLET. It happens, Mick.

MICK. Don't wanna watch it though, do I? Why would I wanna watch women getting knocked about! Load of rubbish. Isn't it? Isn't it?

SCARLET. Well maybe they want people to understand / how –

MICK (*deaf*). Ay?

SCARLET (*louder*). I said maybe they want people to understand how it / can –

MICK. What d'you say?

Beat.

SCARLET. I said yes, Mick.

MICK (*shaking his head as he turns back to the TV*). Not even the real East End, is it? They wanna put something good on. Like that sci-fi film with the bloke in it. Tell you what, that was bloody marvellous. They wanna put something like that on.

LUCY *enters with her large cumbersome suitcase.*

SCARLET. Do you need some help?

LUCY. No, it's fine, it's my own stupid fault for trying to bring it all back in one . . .(*go*).

SCARLET *helps* LUCY *in with the suitcase.*

. . . . Oh, thanks . . .

LUCY *notices* SCARLET*'s silent gesturing and sees* MICK.

Oh, hello dad! What are you doing here?

She goes to kiss him but he swats her away in irritation.

MICK. Been here since five, haven't I?

LUCY (*bemused*). Have you?

MICK (*indignant*). Missed me tea and everything!

LUCY. What are you talking about?

MICK. Five o'clock you said you'd be here! I've been waiting two hours!

LUCY. I never said I'd be back at five, dad . . .

MICK. Yeah. When we spoke last week. I was worried!

LUCY. But . . . ! I never said that! I might have said I had to get *up* at five to get the plane / but . . .

MICK. No, you said you'd be back at five. On the phone, when we spoke.

LUCY. *When* on the phone?

MICK. Well, I don't know. Monday.

LUCY. I hadn't even booked the *flight* on Monday, dad. I didn't book it till yesterday.

MICK. Well, I don't know. You told me sometime. I was worried, wasn't I?

SCARLET *rolls her eyes as she leaves with her pile of things.*

LUCY (*sighs*). Well, I'm here now.

MICK. Just wanted someone to take my mind off things and now my own daughter starts on me.

LUCY. I'm not starting on you. What things?

MICK. Don't matter.

LUCY. What things, dad?

MICK (*shakes his head and sighs*). I just . . . you know, I got bills coming in from all sides. I've had to cash in me pension. The VAT man's after me for six grand, and I don't know which way to turn, do I?

And now I've got this pain.

LUCY. What pain?

MICK (*shakes his head*). Nothing.

LUCY. What pain, dad?

MICK. Here. In me heart. And across here.

He indicates across his chest.

And sort of down me back . . . and arms . . . and . . .

Oh that's right, laugh at me. Just 'cause I'm gonna have a heart attack! Got the VAT man on me back and me cooker's broken down and now I'm gonna have a heart attack and you think it's bloody funny. That's nice again, isn't it?

LUCY. I don't think it's funny. I just . . . don't think there's anything wrong with your heart. You just . . . drink too much. Look, if you're worried, why don't you go to the doctors. I'll come with you if you like.

MICK. And have that sodding woman poke me around again? Not likely.

LUCY. Go to the hospital then. Do you want me to make an appointment?

Long pause.

MICK. Well, I can't now, can I? How can I go now? Got no bloody time to do anything. All this worrying about money. And your yank moving over.

LUCY *sighs, then hesitantly –*

LUCY. Have you thought any more about what I said? About getting a lodger? I think I might know someone . . . he's really nice . . .

Silence. Then MICK *turns with a beaming false smile.*

MICK. So when's he coming then? Your Joe?

LUCY. He's coming on Thursday.

MICK. Tuesday?

LUCY. *Thursday.*

MICK. Thursday, is it? Late as that? Have to come round for dinner.

Beat.

LUCY. That would be nice. Thank you.

MICK. Nice bit of lamb. Few spuds. Some Yorkshires.

LUCY. You'll have to get your cooker fixed first though, won't you?

MICK. Ay?

LUCY. You'll have to get your cooker fixed.

MICK. What you on about?! I don't mean *me*, do I? I'm saying *I'll* have to come round for dinner here.

LUCY. Right.

MICK. Give him a bit of a welcome.

LUCY. Right. Not on Thursday, though?

MICK. Make him feel at home.

LUCY. Dad? You don't mean on Thursday when he's just arrived?

MICK. Ay?

LUCY. You don't mean on *Thursday*?

MICK. Well he'll want a bit of company, won't he?

LUCY. Not when he's just arrived! He'll have been on a plane all day. We haven't seen each other for ages!

MICK. You've only just come back!

LUCY. I was out there for three days! I was just getting my / stuff!

MICK. Oh, alright then. If you don't wanna let him out.

LUCY. It's not about letting him out. Joe can do what he likes. I'm just saying, give us a chance!

MICK. Just trying to help. Got it wrong again, have I?

LUCY. We'll have dinner another time.

Soon.

Ok?

Long beat.

MICK. Yeah, whatever, mate.

MICK *stands.*

LUCY. Dad? You do *like* Joe, don't you?

MICK. Ay?

LUCY. Joe. You do like him?

MICK. It's not up to me, is it mate?

LUCY. No, but . . . I want to know. It's important.

MICK. Yeah, you know. Seems alright.

Well, I don't really *know* him, do I, babe?

LUCY. I really think it's going to work. I think we've got something . . . special.

MICK. Yeah? That right?

He chuckles to himself.

LUCY. What does that mean?

MICK (*still laughing*). Special, have you? Yeah, alright. If you say so.

LUCY. Look, just because it didn't work out for you, doesn't mean it can't / for –

MICK. No. No. (*He laughs again.*) 'Special'. You'll learn . . . Better off on your own. We all are.

LUCY. Yes, well maybe I don't want to be!

SCARLET *catches the end of this as she returns lugging a huge old backpack, now in just a long, baggy tee shirt.*

MICK. Use your loo.

As he leaves SCARLET *gives* LUCY *a sympathetic smile.* LUCY *sighs.*

SCARLET. Welcome home.

LUCY. Sorry. I didn't mean to inflict him on you.

SCARLET. Oh, he's alright. I think he gets worse when you're here. So?! How was it? Joe all ready for the big move?

LUCY. I think so. I can't believe we've got this far, can you?

SCARLET. No last minute doubts? Cold feet? Sudden realisation he's Roman Polanski? Probably best not to think about it . . . Anyway, listen, I think I'm gonna get going . . .

LUCY. But?! He won't be here till next week! You might as
well stay till then?

SCARLET. Nnnn . . . you know me. I get restless . . .

LUCY. Well, where will you go?

SCARLET. I dunno. Somewhere. To my future. Here, look, do
you want these? I can't fit them in.

LUCY. What is it?

SCARLET. Maternity pads and a breast pump. Well, they were
just lying around the office and, you know, they're
expensive. All baby stuff is. It's such a rip off.

No? I just thought . . . Joe and everything? No. Not yet
then. Oh well . . .

She resumes trying to stuff them into the over-packed bag.

LUCY. Look Scarlet, you will come next week, won't you?
When Joe's here? I don't want to lose you . . . Oh! And
I want to hear about your course!

SCARLET. Er . . . No. Actually I decided that wasn't right.

LUCY. What do you mean? I thought you really wanted it! You
did all that work!

SCARLET. Yeah, no I . . . decided . . . You know Lucy, I just
don't think college is the right answer for me.

Hey! I read my horoscope this morning! It said, 'an eventful
week'. Do you think that means emotionally or physically?

She looks down at the remaining clothes in her hand.

I better wear jeans just in case . . .

As SCARLET *starts putting on her jeans,* MICK *comes
back in and beams. To* LUCY –

MICK. Right. See you Thursday then. Come about seven,
shall I?

SCARLET *takes her backpack and turns to the audience.*

SCARLET. A week before this I was getting ready to go and
enrol. Lucy was geeing me up as usual – she can be really
smug sometimes, what I should be doing with my life and
all that stuff – I've known her since I was four, so you can't
get away from it. We used to joke that if a man didn't fancy
one of us, he'd fancy the other because we're such physical
opposites, we're like chalk and cheese, although Lucy

always says I have to be the chalk because I'm tall and brittle, and she's the cheese 'cause she's fat. She's not yellow though.

Anyway I'd been moaning on as usual about some pointless fucking job I was doing, selling sanitary towel dispensers to middle-aged, company bosses and how I can't speak any more. I've got nothing to say . . . and Lucy starts on about how she thinks I *can* speak and that I'm creative and that maybe I should find a way to *harness* it. So we find these brochures for the technical college and there's this course called 'Finding Your Voice' and it all just suddenly makes sense.

So last week, it was the enrolment, so I put on something that made me look vaguely intelligent, a bit more 'political animal' than someone who sits in the lay-by binge eating Mars Bars, and I was really pleased with myself because I left the house in loads of time and I was just getting close . . . when I suddenly realised I was *hungry*.

'Course, all there is is these disgusting little kebab shops and burger places down there – stupid frazzled crap on sticks and bits of rat – and I'm not eating that. Meat's really bad for your psychic abilities. And Buddhists don't eat it. My friend Sharon's a Buddhist. She used to be a clubber but she gave it all up to go and live in the hills and eat mealy meal. Or whatever it is. Apparently they have to say Buddha three thousand times a day. I said to her, 'That's a lot of times to say Buddha' and she said, 'Yes, it *is* a lot of times and I didn't see the point of it really, but then I had this really amazing experience . . . ' And *I've* never had a really amazing experience – except once maybe, on Brighton beach, but then I had been smoking spliff for hours . . . so I suppose she's got a point . . .

Anyway I'm getting in a foul mood because I can't find anything even half edible, and this hole in my stomach's beginning to eat away at me, and then finally, after what feels like about three days and I'm all sweaty and swearing when I wanted to be *together*, I get to this bookshop. One of those chains that has a café in it so you can squish carrot cake into books and tip coffee all over them and then not buy them . . .

. . . Anyway, I haven't got time for any of that now as I've only got twenty minutes left to enrol, so I get in the queue for the bagels and double decaff exploit-the-third-world latte, and I wait.

The woman in front of me is whittering on about some *wheat* intolerance like she's really fucking proud of it, and it's making my head hurt, so I turn to face Jewish Studies just to shut her noise out.

I notice this man, blond, twatty-looking with a built-in sneer. Arran jumper deal, you know the type. Probably lives in my mum's village with a wife all draped in linen and a brood of horrible brats. *Judgemental looking.*

As I get closer, I see the book he's reading is on the holocaust, and it's open at a picture of a woman who looks like Lucy, wearing a yellow star. And just for a moment, I'm distracted because it strikes me as strange to use something as lovely as a star to stigmatise someone, when you think of stars as being like gold, like fame, or like the sun. And it's the star that sticks in my mind as, half an hour later, in his Poggenpohl, just 'off-white' kitchen, he sticks himself into my body and I make like a porn queen with one foot on his wife's Ideal Home magazines and the other in the cat litter tray.

Afterwards he looks a little dazed. He peels himself off, wipes himself with a tissue and tells me his name is Richard. I say I'm Judy. He doesn't get the joke. And from the smug inanity of his expression he has not one fucking notion that right now I want to put a poker through his head and keep on smashing until his 'architecturally designed dream-house' has a scarlet water feature.

Instead, I smile politely as he asks me if I came. 'Yes,' I lie. And he believes me. 'I'm starving. What have you got that I can eat?'.

Scene Four.

LUCY *and* GABRIEL *stand on a rattling tube train, holding the rail.*

LUCY. But you know what I mean, though?

GABRIEL (*pulls a face*). I can't honestly say I've ever actually wanted to jump under a tube train, no.

LUCY. No, I mean, I don't mean to actually kill yourself. But the feeling.

The rush as the train comes in. I just mean you can understand the impulse. Like, you know how we're supposed to be attracted to things we fear . . . I saw this documentary once, about families living in Beirut, and they didn't have to stay but they did. Because they got addicted to the destruction. They found it beautiful . . .

Beat.

GABRIEL. All I can say is, it's a very good job I'm coming with you to the airport.

LUCY (*laughs*). Only so you can get your luggage.

He smiles. They're fond of each other.

GABRIEL. So go on then, explain to me how that works, that your dad sells cars and you can't drive? Doesn't it strike you as a bit odd?

LUCY. I suspect it's deeply Freudian. So what does yours do? Make luggage?

GABRIEL. No, he's just an arsehole. My sister told him I raped her and he believed her.

LUCY. Wow, that's hard!

GABRIEL. Yeah, well. You can't blame her. She's pretty sick, she's a junkie. And he's an arsehole . . .

Beat.

Still, at least he's not as deaf as yours.

LUCY. Are you getting on alright with him?

GABRIEL. Yeah. Fine. He's a bit of a tricky bastard but I'm getting the hang of him.

LUCY. I'm glad he's got some company. Especially at the minute, with Joe coming and everything.

GABRIEL. Keep him out your hair, eh?

LUCY. No, I didn't mean that. I just . . .

I hope he'll be alright with Joe. It's funny, you know? I've just always really trusted that it would work out. Do you know what I mean? It felt fated. Do you believe in that?

GABRIEL. Errrr . . . ?

LUCY. You'll think it's silly . . .

GABRIEL. No, go on.

LUCY. It's just, right from the beginning. It felt like . . . signs.

GABRIEL. What? Like . . . 'Lucy . . . ' (*He points to his head with both hands.*) . . . 'Shag This Man'?

She gives him a look, then smiles.

LUCY. I just mean . . . New York kept coming up. And then one of my sculptures got chosen for an exhibition there – this huge self portrait made out of junk – and so I had to go over. And I felt so free . . . you know, when you feel like you're radiating light? And Joe came and stood next to me. Something in his eyes . . . something . . .

I just mean there were all these coincidences. Like that book, the Celestine Prophesy. Do you know what I mean?

GABRIEL. Errrr . . . pass! I'm just a stupid Kiwi. I don't know about stuff like that.

LUCY. No, you're not. Stupid I mean. You're *obviously* not.

GABRIEL. You are pretty clever though, aren't you?

LUCY. No. I'm just normal. Sorry, anyway. I'm being boring. I'm ranting . . .

GABRIEL. No you're not. (*Beat.*) What does Joe think?

LUCY. Joe?

GABRIEL. Does he believe in fate?

LUCY (*smiles*). No. Joe thinks we make our own future.

She laughs.

Joe says I'm too negative. He says I always see the bad stuff and dwell on it, that I'll always think of the worse case scenario and that by doing that I bring it towards me. Like when he's ill, I'll ask if he's feeling better and he gets angry because he doesn't want to think about the fact that he's ill. He thinks it's weakness. So he pretends it's not happening. But I think it's important to face up to things. At least then you're prepared if something really bad happens.

Joe thinks I'm stupid.

Beat.

GABRIEL. Joe thinks pretending an illness isn't there makes it go away?

LUCY. Yes. So what do you think?

GABRIEL. I don't really think about things like that. I just get on with it. I don't think about the future.

They exit the train and head towards the terminal.

So what happened with your sculpture? Did you sell it?

LUCY. No. (*Laughs.*) There was a problem during shipment and it arrived all covered in cheese. Some export had leaked. It was disgusting.

But it didn't matter, because I got Joe.

Do you know, he's not afraid of dying? I'm petrified of it, but Joe doesn't even care. It's one of the things I love about him.

GABRIEL. I'm not scared of dying either.

LUCY. Aren't you?

GABRIEL. Nope. Coz I'm never gonna die . . .

LUCY *laughs but then suddenly reacts as she sees someone ahead.*

LUCY. Oh my God, he's there already! Look! Joe! Joe?!

GABRIEL *looks as* LUCY *charges over to a tall, good-looking American:* JOE.

JOE. Heeyyyyy!! Baby!

GABRIEL *watches as they kiss and hug.*

Scene Five.

LUCY*'s bedroom.*

JOE *enters with his suitcase, followed a little nervously by* LUCY.

LUCY. Welcome home.

JOE *puts his suitcase on the bed and nods, digesting this as he looks around.*

LUCY. This is weird. I can't believe you're really here.

JOE. Oh yeah, baby! In the flesh! (*He laughs.*) Although it was pretty touch and go for a while!!

LUCY. What do you mean?

JOE. Uh, I didn't tell you. This morning!

I wake up, half an hour before the flight, totally steaming, and I'm like 'shit!' So I'm straight in a cab and I get to the check in, my eyeballs bleeding down my face, and I throw my ticket at this woman, and she looks at me and says, 'I shouldn't be letting you on this flight, boarding has finished'.

And I just can't say anything, just look at her like I'm half dead, and she says, 'But I'm going to upgrade you to first class and get you on,' and I just nod, like, 'Yeah, whatever,' and she looks at me and says 'Do you understand what I'm doing for you?' And I'm like . . . 'Uuh?' and she's like, 'Do you even know who you *are*?'.

He laughs again.

LUCY. Good leaving party then.

JOE. *Oh* yeah. Oh yeah. Uh, it was disgusting! How much did we drink?!

LUCY (*smiles*). Who came?

JOE. Everyone.

But he nods and looks away. A slight tension.

So Mom sends her love and some cookies and all the guys said to say hi. And that they can't believe I'm going off to live in London with a beautiful English girl. But you know, I told 'em, 'I love Lucy!'.

LUCY *looks fleetingly uncertain. He comes over and kisses her.*

LUCY. Oh! Erm . . . my *dad's* coming for dinner tonight. I'm really sorry. I tried to put him off but he wouldn't take the hint . . .

JOE. It's fine. Bring him on!

Beat. LUCY *nods but seems slightly disappointed. She moves away.*

LUCY. So what do you want to do? I've cleared out half the wardrobe and these drawers – I had too much stuff anyway . . . Oh! And we've got a shower! It's a bit cranky but . . .

Do you think you're gonna like it here?

JOE. *I* am gonna have a great time in *old*, funny, little England. And I'm gonna eat spotted dick, and 'take the mickey' and drive cars with boots and bonnets, and learn to say . . . (*Cockney accent.*) 'Alright mate' . . . and order pints and everything is just gonna be 'brilliant!'.

LUCY. Do you remember, our first night in New York? You took me to that funny little dive bar. But I didn't have any ID . . .

JOE. And you said that if they didn't believe you were over twenty-one you'd show them your saggy tits to prove it.

LUCY. Is that really what made you like me?

JOE. You had a beautiful accent, and sparkly eyes, and I looked at you and I thought, 'This girl has got it going on'.

LUCY. And then when the bar shut I said, 'Whaddayamean, *shut*?! This is supposed to be the city that never sleeps!' And you said we could go to Central Park to look at the stars . . .

But JOE *just moves over to kiss her.*

It's weird, isn't it? Do you feel weird?

JOE. No, baby. Just horny.

LUCY. Oh no! We don't have to do the sex thing again, do we?

JOE (*unravelling her top*). I'm afraid so. But then afterwards you can do something *you* like.

LUCY. Like cleaning?

JOE. Yes baby, afterwards you can do the cleaning.

LUCY *smiles at their familiar joke.*

LUCY. It's weird, when we haven't been together for a while, it's like you close up and become round instead of having a bit that attaches and connects to the other one.

JOE *is deadpan as he looks down.*

JOE. I've still got a bit that attaches. Look, it's right here.

A long moment as they start to get into it, JOE *unravelling her clothes more and more. Then suddenly* LUCY *bursts into tears.* JOE *pulls back, puzzled.*

JOE. What's the matter?

LUCY. Nothing. I don't know.

She wipes her eyes.

I think I'm just . . . pleased to see you.

Scene Six

LUCY*'s living room / dining room.*

MICK *drinks beer from a can as he closely watches a TV science programme, sitting in the black swivel chair.* JOE, *also with a beer, half watches from a little further away.* SCARLET *opens wine at the table.*

TV NARRATOR. . . . the most destructive objects in the galaxy are born from the deaths of the brightest stars, and when these massive stars become too heavy, they implode to form Black Holes.

> LUCY *enters and smiles at* SCARLET *as she places a serving bowl of vegetables on the table.*

LUCY. Thanks.

TV NARRATOR. Any star unlucky enough to stray too close to a Black Hole will cross its Event Horizon . . . and become caught in the Black Hole's immense gravitational pull . . . From this point on, it's certain future is to be destroyed by the singularity at the Black Hole's centre where gravity is infinitely strong and all known laws of time and space break down.

> *Without stopping,* LUCY *does a circuit of* MICK *and* JOE, *collecting empty cans, then returns to the kitchen.*

TV NARRATOR. Like most predators, Black Holes leave a trail of destruction behind them, and in fact because they give out no light, we can only tell they're there at all by the havoc they create.

> MICK *crushes a beer can.* LUCY *hurries back out with potatoes, followed by* GABRIEL, *at his own pace, carrying the carved joint of lamb.* SCARLET *is very aware of him.*

LUCY. Does anyone need more beer?

> MICK *indicates he does. She nods.*

GABRIEL (*to* LUCY). Where do you want this?

LUCY. Oh, anywhere. Thanks. Joe? Do you want one?

JOE. Yeah, sure.

TV NARRATOR. If you want to find a Black Hole, you have to look for stars that have become caught in their immense gravitational pull . . . and are being hurled around at impossible speeds as the black hole feeds on them.

LUCY *hurries back to the kitchen.*

SCARLET (*to* GABRIEL). Where are you sitting? I know, have this one 'cause it's nice and . . . a long way from the door . . .

SCARLET *fills a glass for him in the seat nearest hers.*

SCARLET. Joe can go at the head . . .

JOE *turns to the table as* SCARLET *fills his glass* (*which is furthest away from her*).

JOE. Hey, this looks great!

LUCY (*coming back in*). I'm not sure actually, it's probably a bit . . . overdone . . .

SCARLET (*to* GABRIEL). I can't even cook!

But GABRIEL *is watching* JOE *as he sits.* LUCY *busies about, checking everything.*

TV NARRATOR. This deadly embrace will last / many millions of years until . . .

LUCY. Go for it. Don't let it get cold. Dad? Dinner.

MICK. Lovely.

MICK *finally turns from the TV and comes to take his place at the table, having a good, proprietorial peer at what's on offer first, and still trying to watch the TV over everyone's heads. Everyone helps themselves as* LUCY *turns it off and puts some music on quietly instead.*

SCARLET *continues to look at* GABRIEL. JOE *digs into the food.*

SCARLET. Well this is a bit grown up . . . !

JOE. I am *ravenous* . . .

GABRIEL. They didn't feed you on the plane?

JOE *laughs.*

JOE. As a matter of fact, there's a funny story about that . . .

LUCY (*laughs as she sits*). Oh, this is hilarious! Scarlet, listen to this!

JOE. Ok, so I'm sitting on the plane, and I've got one of those little menus they give you, to tell you what's available? So I look at it, and it's like beef . . . or lasagne. So this guy comes down the plane, the steward, and he's handing out food and you can tell he's gay, you know, his hair and his manner and stuff. And he keeps looking at me, you know, like, he likes me. So then he gets to me and he says, 'Now. Would you like beef? Or vagina?'.

SCARLET *starts to laugh.* MICK *continues to eat as if he isn't listening.*

SCARLET. No! He really said that?

JOE. So then he goes, 'Did I just say that? I can't believe I just said that.' And I said, 'Yup, you just said that.'.

GABRIEL. So what did you go for?

JOE. Vagina. I didn't want there to be any misunderstandings.

SCARLET. I love that.

LUCY. I think it's hysterical when people do those things subconsciously and say what they're / really –

MICK (*interrupts suddenly*). You tasted this lamb, Joe? Lovely bit of meat that is. Got that from the butcher's up the road. You like lamb?

Beat.

JOE. Ah, yeah. Yeah. It's good. I was uh, I was actually telling a story there, Mick.

MICK *pours himself a large glass of wine.*

MICK. So what do you think of old Londinium then, Joe?

LUCY. Dad!

But JOE *shakes his head at her, it's OK.*

JOE. Yeah, it's a great new opportunity. I'm looking forward to living here.

MICK. Eh?

JOE. I'm very excited about living here . . . and learning Cockney rhyming slang.

MICK. Oh yeah? Old boat race? Apples and pears? Merchant banker?

He cackles to himself.

JOE. All of that.

MICK. Trouble and strife. Jimmy riddle.

JOE. Yep.

MICK. Pearly gates. How's your father. Dog and duck.

LUCY. Yes, thank you, Mr Entertainer.

MICK. Well, he wants to know, doesn't he? He just said. I dunno, answer a question and you get your head bitten off round here! That's bloody nice again, isn't it?

GABRIEL. You *were* going on a bit, Mick.

MICK (*to* LUCY). Ay? What d'you say? You what?

LUCY. You were just . . . Don't show off in front of Joe, dad. He's only just got here . . .

MICK. Charming, isn't it?! See what I get? Be your turn next, Joe. You wanna watch out.

LUCY. He's got nothing to watch out for! I'm just saying . . .

Beat.

SCARLET. So, erm, what are you doing in England then, Gabriel?

GABRIEL. I'm travelling.

JOE (*glad someone's asked*). Travelling? Yeah? What, like, on vacation, you mean?

MICK. It's getting like the bloody United Nations round here.

LUCY (*to* SCARLET). He's been in Vietnam, Scarlet. The exact same village we stayed in! Do you remember, the / one where . . .

SCARLET. Oh my God, and I had that motorbike and I was . . . !

She turns to GABRIEL *about to tell him.*

GABRIEL. Have you been there Joe?

JOE. Uh. Not there. (*Beat.*) We were in France though, last April. That was cool . . .

SCARLET. Oh God, don't! I was renovating that house for that horrible old . . . ! (*She laughs, to* GABRIEL.) I was trying to get the workmen to varnish a beam, and I got this idea into my head that I was Mrs Native French Speaker, so I said, 'Eh . . . Monsieur, si vous . . . preservatif . . . sur le pute . . . dans la plafond' and he just sort of legged it. And it turned out I'd asked him to hang a condom from the whore on the ceiling!

GABRIEL *smiles.*

GABRIEL. Shouldn't think they'd mind that in France . . .

MICK. You still thinking of moving out there then, Scarlet? To Frogland?

SCARLET (*shifts uncomfortably*). Uh, no, actually I decided . . . Well . . . (*To* LUCY.) Richard's given me a flat to stay in and I don't have to pay for it, / so . . .

MICK. Who's Richard then?

LUCY (*shaking her head*). Her new boyfriend.

JOE. Oh yeah?

MICK *rolls his eyes, typical.*

SCARLET (*glances at* GABRIEL). Well, I wouldn't *exactly* say he's / my . . .

MICK (*interrupting*). Do you know Joe, when I left school I was gonna be a scientist. You know that? Applied for a job in space research.

Beat. JOE *holds out his hand to stay* LUCY.

JOE. No, I . . . didn't know that . . .

MICK *finishes his wine again.*

MICK. But my trouble was, I liked women too much, and if you wanna keep a woman you've gotta have money. And scientists don't earn any.

SCARLET. Some of them do if / they're . . .

He takes something out of his pocket and shows it to JOE.

MICK. What do you think that is then, Joe?

JOE. I uh . . .

MICK. No. *Look* at it. Look properly and tell me what you think it is.

JOE. I've . . . no idea. I don't know.

MICK. That is a piece of metal that's been round the moon. That was from the Apollo spacecraft. To dream of space. To

understand. That's what matters. Can you imagine that, Joe?
Looking into the heavens? Finding out the answers to how
and why we're here? We came out of a black hole, did you
know that? And we're going to end up back in one.

Do you read, Joe?

JOE. Read?

MICK. Novels. Science fiction. You should read, 'A Brief
History of Time'. I'll lend it to you.

JOE. Right.

MICK. It's all about that, the beginning and the end. That's
what's important. Not all this buying a bigger house and
filling it full of stuff, not your going to church every Sunday
just to feel better about what you've bloody done.

LUCY. Dad . . . don't . . .

MICK. What? What daughter? Bossy cow, she is, isn't she?

GABRIEL (*sotto voce to* LUCY). Do you want me to take him
home and lock him in?

    LUCY *smiles, but* JOE *frowns.*

MICK. Cor, tell you what, bloody vegetarians can't cook
vegetables, can they? These are so hard I just cut me lip!

SCARLET. I think they're / lovely . . .

LUCY. Someone take a photo of my dad, he's cut his lip!

MICK. Well, they're hard. Aren't they, Joe? I mean, are these
hard or are they hard?

JOE (*still distracted by* GABRIEL). They are a bit on the
crunchy side.

    MICK *laughs.*

MICK. See what I mean! I tell you how I like 'em. All soft and
mushy, so you can mash 'em into your spuds. Lovely that.
Not like these. She wants to break me bleeding teeth as well
as me having a heart attack.

LUCY. I told you to go to the hospital!

    MICK, *now quite drunk, growls and shakes his head. Then
    looks at* LUCY *all innocent.*

MICK. Just making a comment, babe. Oh alright, I see. Shut
up dad. Got it wrong again, have I?

The clicking of forks. A long beat.

JOE. So . . . you're living with Mick are you, Gabriel?

GABRIEL. For a while.

LUCY. Oh! Yes! It just sort of helps them both out really . . .
It seemed like a good –

GABRIEL. Lucy found me at the airport.

LUCY. Well, no . . . not really! (*To* JOE.) I was . . . *sick* . . .
actually . . .

JOE *frowns, unimpressed.*

GABRIEL. Lucy says you work in insurance?

JOE *gives her a worse look.*

JOE. Uh! I'm a . . . Risk Management Consultant. For a large . . .
company.

SCARLET. Euch! Adding up . . . ! That's something I'm
allergic to!

LUCY *smiles.*

GABRIEL. An insurance company?

JOE *smiles yes.*

SCARLET (*sensing a tension, still flirting*). God, and
insurance! I've had too many disasters, I'd never get cover!
Can I have another potato?

MICK *passes them to her as* LUCY *indicates the meat.*

LUCY. Does anyone want more –

MICK. Seen your mum, have you?

LUCY. Dad! That's / no –

MICK. Ay? What d'you say? Ay?

LUCY. I've *spoken* to her.

MICK. She still with that wanker? Bloody butcher's shop! She
was all Watership Sodding Down when we were together,
now she's hacking the bastards to pieces!

LUCY. She's *happy*, dad.

MICK. Grrr . . .

LUCY. She is.

MICK. I tell you what, that woman . . . !

LUCY. Please don't.

MICK. 'Don't'? *Don't?* What d'you want me to do?

To JOE *and* GABRIEL.

I tell you what, don't trust 'em! Only ever been with two women in my life, I have, Lucy's mother and one other one before her . . .

LUCY. Dad, please!

SCARLET. Er, Mick . . .

MICK. . . . and they both give me a disease. Do you know that? Both of them go off with some other wanker, and both come back and give me some sod / ding . . .

LUCY. The doctor said there's no such thing! He said there's something called . . . what you said it was called, but it doesn't do what you said!

MICK. Sick as a dog. In fear of me life. Laid out on me back.

LUCY. It wasn't her fault!

MICK. Weeks I was there! (*To* LUCY.) I got a reaction! Arthritis, didn't I? You remember, Scarlet. They said, if I ever got it again, I'd be crippled for life. That's what they said! So I don't wanna know about women, do I! Steer clear! Isn't that what I say, Lucy? Better off on your own!

An awkward silence. LUCY *glances with concern at* JOE *then looks away.*

LUCY. I'm sorry about my dad, he's had too much to drink . . .

MICK. You what?

GABRIEL. It's alright, Lucy . . .

MICK. Embarrassed you, have I? Daddy in the dog house? Being too heavy? Only saying what's true, aren't I, babe? Only making a comment.

Oh, alright then. I see.

GABRIEL. Yeah, let's leave it now though Mick, yeah?

But MICK *starts to sing as though to cheer* LUCY *up.*

MICK. The sun has got his hat on, hip hip hip hooray, the sun has got his hat on and he's coming out to play. Now we'll all be happy, hip hip hip hooray . . .

SCARLET. Mick . . .

She gives him a warning look.

MICK. What? Whassamatter?

An awkward beat. Then to JOE *and* GABRIEL –

SCARLET. Did Lucy tell you about her new commission? It's for the hospital. They chose her out of five hundred artists!

JOE. Er, no.

SCARLET (*to* GABRIEL). Have you seen her work, Gabriel? It's really clever. She makes sculptures out of . . . well, you tell them, Lucy. You can explain it best.

She . . . she finds things that other people have chucked out . . . that they think is rubbish . . . and she makes them into art. That's roughly right, isn't it?

LUCY *nods.*

GABRIEL. Yeah, I was trying to get her to show me but . . .

You keep getting out of it, don't you?

As LUCY *concedes a smile,* SCARLET *clocks this, realising that* GABRIEL *is interested in* LUCY.

SCARLET. Yeah, I'm not creative at all. I'm just –

JOE. Yeah, I've been looking forward to seeing what she's working on.

SCARLET. It's got some space theme, hasn't it? See Mick, even you'd like it.

MICK. Would I? (*Laughing.*) Yeah, alright . . .

SCARLET. Well, the hospital really love it. / They –

MICK. Don't matter what they love though, does it? You can love what you like but it's the money that counts.

LUCY. No, not with the hospital. It's more of a prestige / thing . . .

MICK. Well, that don't pay the bills, does it! (*To* JOE.) Cor, I bet your company would have something to say about it if you said you haven't brought them in any money this year, but you've got 'em some prestige!

JOE. Yeah, I think you could be right there, Mick!

MICK. I haven't made any money, but I've got us lots of friends! The almighty dollar. That's what it's all about!

Survival of the fittest. Hey, tell you what, Joe. Do you like sport?

JOE. I do as it happens.

MICK. Snooker?

JOE. Uh . . . I play pool . . . ?

MICK. No. S'different. No strategy in pool. Snooker's all about strategy. I'll take you down my club, teach you how to play.

JOE (*very aware of* GABRIEL). Yeah, I'd like that.

MICK. Pot the black.

JOE. That'd be great.

MICK. We'll put you down for a membership.

JOE. Well thanks.

LUCY. Does anyone want / more . . .

MICK. I'll tell you what, we could get down there now, if you like? Still got an hour before they shut.

JOE. Uh . . .

LUCY. Dad . . .

MICK. Introduce you to the blokes. Get you in there.

JOE (*glances at* GABRIEL). Well, I . . .

MICK (*laughing*). Well don't look at him! I'm not taking him! He can't even hit the damn thing!

SCARLET. How *many* blokes . . . ?

LUCY. Dad!

MICK (*to* JOE). Unless you . . . *particularly wanna* have afters . . . ?

JOE. It's alright, Lucy. (*Beat.*) Uh, no. Sure. Why not? (*To* LUCY.) You don't mind, do you.

MICK. 'Course she don't. You're here for good now, aren't you? She's got all the time in the world.

He kisses LUCY *on the cheek.*

Alright mate. See you later.

JOE (*also kisses her*). See you later, Lucy.

MICK *and* JOE *leave, already chatting.*

LUCY. Um, well! Bye then.

SCARLET. At least they get on.

LUCY looks fed up. GABRIEL grins and gives her a playful nudge.

GABRIEL. I can have Joe's.

SCARLET. Ooh, yes! More for us! Spotted dick and custard . . . !

LUCY laughs as SCARLET gets up to get it.

GABRIEL. Yeah, thanks Luce. (*He squeezes her.*) You're a star.

Lights go down on the table and up on SCARLET, as she moves towards us.

SCARLET. Lucy and I used to play Crap Family Poker. Lucy would call a Bullying-Father and a Mother-On-Valium, and I'd match her Mother-On-Valium and raise her a Bastard-Stepfather-Who-Charges-Me-Rent. Although, when I was thirteen he put it up to more than I could earn with a Saturday job, so I had to move out . . .

Actually, it might have had something to do with me telling the neighbours I'd caught him trying to shag the living room carpet . . . Anyway, he and darling mother decided I was surplus to requirements, so I went to live with Lucy.

It was a funny set-up. Mick was never there or when he was he was just drunk the whole time, belting out 'You Won't Find Another Fool Like Me,' at three in the morning and Lucy's mum, Geraldine, was always round the cooker as if for warmth, going round and round in circles.

I used to feel guilty, and I didn't want to be in the way, so I'd help her and when I did, she had a really lovely smile. Like sunshine. 'Cept mostly she'd be crying, or whispering into the phone – *obviously* having an affair, though Lucy couldn't see it and I wasn't gonna be the one to tell her.

Lucy and I were not exactly your well-adjusted teenagers at the time. She was in her gothic we're-all-going-to-die-of-AIDS-phase and I was just more interested in . . . planting a bomb in my mother's tampon, I suppose.

We'd pass on the landing in the mornings, me on my way to be sick after binge eating too much cereal, and her on her way to steal money from her dad's wallet.

Lucy hated Mick. Or rather, I think she tried to hate him because he never really took any notice of her. Except to say 'Don't like boys too much, you're better off on your own'. I think she thought it was her *fault* somehow. Then she found his stash of porn magazines that were full of tall, pouty women with big tits and somehow took it as an explanation . . .

I remember her showing them to me, all contemptuously, and laughing at the 'stupid women' but I could see she was upset. I think she thought I was part of the conspiracy, she kept saying I looked like them . . . and weren't they disgusting?

Although I've never thought porn magazines *were* disgusting actually. You can sort of understand them, can't you? These women looking at you, just asking to be fucked. It makes you want to be a man yourself so you can do it too . . . fuck 'em really hard . . . or maybe just punch them in the gut . . .

But that wasn't what I was talking about, was it . . . See? I'm crap. I can't talk any more . . . I don't know what I'm saying, I start on these stories and they don't have an end . . .

Oh yeah, that's right, so Lucy would steal his money, and then she'd go on huge shopping sprees and buy . . . oh I don't know . . . *clothes* . . . Mostly she never wore them or she'd just throw them away, except this one dress . . . ! Oh my God, it was awful, a huge yellow silk thing, the colour of . . . human fat! It looked like a parachute . . .

So this one morning Lucy's in a snit because her dad's got up early for once, *avec* wallet, so she comes downstairs for breakfast but her dad bangs into her and tells her she can't come down like that – what if one of his friends came round?

'Course, Mick's just freaked out at having a teenage daughter on the loose with no knickers on, no matter how long her dressing gown is, but Lucy immediately takes it as final proof that she's too repulsive to be seen in public, so she comes running back upstairs and shoves her face in a line of my speed to take the edge off things.

I thought of going to her, but at that point I was still cross because she'd shrunk my new top so . . .

Anyway, so the big scene between Lucy and Mick gives Geraldine the perfect excuse to pick a fight so she can nip out for a quick one, so she throws a hissy fit, like a little girl, and storms out, saying she's had enough of the lot of them and isn't ever coming back. Which starts Lucy off crying and screaming and . . .

Which, of course, is really hard to wank through, so I finally give up and come out onto the landing to see if I can help. I bump into a lodger, a grey-skinned man with eyes like a lizard, carrying a suitcase. He tells me he's leaving. All this shouting is too much to put up with. And he misses his wife. So he's going somewhere with a video machine in his room. So he can watch videos. Because he's lonely.

I see him look me up and down, and I know what he's thinking. And Geraldine's been good to me and she needs the money.

Penises are strange. On one level, mechanics. But on the other, a manifest wanting of me. And it's the wanting that sucks me in, holding it up to the light like a marble, to look at, in awe, this penis-shaped wanting of me.

And while he grunts in the darkness, lost in his skin, I gaze at my marble. And later, I have black acorns in my stomach, acorns of anger and despising how easily that desire for me was sated. And I plant them and watch them grow into big dark trees hiding me from the light.

Downstairs the front door goes as Geraldine comes back. The grey-skinned lodger strokes my skin, eying up the one remaining hole he hasn't been in. 'You dirty girl,' he whispers. 'You've got 'Fuck me' written all over you. You want me in here, don't you?' 'Yes,' I lie. But what I'm really thinking is, it's seven o'clock. Which means I've missed dinner.

Scene Seven.

Office at airport. Sounds of planes landing outside.

JOE *eating a sandwich, enters and moves to the phone. He dials.*

JOE. Hey! It's me. How you doing?

No, I can't talk long, I'm at the airport.

No, I'm not coming home! I'm working! We've got the contract here, with the airline! Andy said I could use his phone to call you.

Hey mom, I'm a grown up, I can do that. No, I'm not sneaking around.

Yeah, no, good. Good. She's fine. She sends her love. She's working on a new commission for the hospital to do an artwork. Yes, she *is* talented.

And *I* am doing great too. I am having a great time and doing well. Everything here is brilliant! It's so easy to be brilliant. You just call up someone for information and they say, 'yeah, that's brilliant' and you're like 'Really?! Just for that?! I'm brilliant? It's *that* easy . . . ?!'.

Yeah, uh, OK.

Hey dad!

Yes, I am. Yes, I have friends. There's this one guy, Gabriel he's called, who's travelling round the world.

No, he's not a salesman, he's just travelling. Like a vacation. But longer.

No, I'm not falling in with the wrong types, he's just . . . Dad, he's just . . .

Annoyed . . .

. . . . Ok dad, put mom back on, would you . . . ?

Cheery again.

Hey!

Then disappointment.

Oh, yeah, OK. Quilting. Alright, I'll talk to you another time.

JOE *hangs up, Irritated. Then he dials again.*

Hey Mick, it's Joe. Yeah. How you doing?

Of *course* it's nice to hear from me! I'm a very funny guy . . . !

Scene Eight.

LUCY*'s garden.*

LUCY *is arranging 'found objects' (mostly rubbish) in a circle, creating a sculpture. She listens to a ghetto blaster and sings and moves along to the Gorillaz 'Useless' in a little world of her own.*

After a minute, GABRIEL *appears from the street, wearing clothes smeared with yellow paint. He smiles as he watches her, then comes up behind her. She jumps.*

LUCY. You made me jump!

GABRIEL. Sorry.

He grins. LUCY *is embarrassed at having been seen dancing and turns the music down.*

GABRIEL. It's a good track.

LUCY. So how are you? Long time, no see.

GABRIEL. Yeah, I've been . . . God knows, clubbing actually. A bit too much. And doing a bit too much e!

LUCY. It's a big scene here.

GABRIEL (*pulls a mock panicked face*). You're not kidding! I thought I better get a job to have some time off it!

LUCY *laughs. He indicates his clothes.*

I'm converting a church into 'luxury apartments'.

LUCY. Oh yeah?

GABRIEL. I brought you this.

He hands her a piece of yellow glass and she peers at it, pleased and fascinated.

LUCY. What is it?!

GABRIEL. It's from the stained glass window. It's actually a nightmare. We've had to chop the church up to put the floors in and you end up having to decide whether to cut Mary's head off, or separate her and Joseph or slice her up the middle . . .

LUCY. So what's this piece?

GABRIEL. I think it's her boob.

LUCY *laughs.*

LUCY. I thought Mary always wore blue?

GABRIEL. Oh, right. It must be a halo then.

LUCY. Thank you. That's funny. A halo from Gabriel.

GABRIEL. So how's it coming along?

LUCY. Oh, getting there. I think.

GABRIEL. Yeah? Great! (*He looks down.*) What's it supposed to be?

LUCY. I don't know. It's not necessarily anything. I mean, I thought I'd do a star . . . but then I sort of got distracted and it turned into a big circle, so now I'm not sure . . .

GABRIEL *nods as he considers it.* LUCY *looks embarrassed.*

Anyway. I don't know. It's probably rubbish.

GABRIEL. I like it.

LUCY. Really?

GABRIEL. Yeah.

LUCY *smiles, grateful.*

LUCY. I thought you were avoiding us.

GABRIEL. Don't be daft, why would I do that?

LUCY. Well. Probably had more than enough of us, living with my dad. You're probably cursing me for getting you into it . . .

GABRIEL. 'Course not.

LUCY. Oh. . . . maybe it's just me then. I'm probably just horrible. Joe gets on alright with him too, actually, so . . .

GABRIEL (*significant*). I saw Joe today.

LUCY. Did you? What, at the airport?

GABRIEL. Yeah. They *still* haven't got my luggage . . .

LUCY (*smiles*). Did you say hello?

GABRIEL. No. He was . . . he looked busy.

LUCY. Yeah, he works hard. He's out there all the time.

Beat. Something he's not telling her.

GABRIEL. I dunno, maybe it wasn't even him. Guys in suits . . . all blend together really, don't they . . .

So, how's things going in the love nest?

LUCY (*nodding*). Good.

She starts to clear her work.

GABRIEL. Yeah?

LUCY. Yeah.

GABRIEL. All completely perfect.

LUCY. Of course.

GABRIEL. Good for you.

LUCY (*smiles*). There's the usual teething problems, but . . . nothing serious.

GABRIEL. Leaving the toilet seat up?

LUCY. No, he's good with that actually. You know, just a few . . . things.

GABRIEL. Making you do all his ironing.

LUCY (*laughs*). No. He gets his shirts dry-cleaned. Just . . . you know, little . . . Nothing important.

GABRIEL. Nothing that a bit of sex can't cure.

LUCY. Absolutely.

GABRIEL. That's the trouble with being single. You never get to have sober sex.

LUCY *laughs.*

LUCY. I'm not sure you do in relationships either.

GABRIEL. Yeah? You're always drunk?

LUCY. Well . . . you know . . .

GABRIEL. You have a good sex life though?

LUCY. Yes.

GABRIEL *nods. Then laughs.*

GABRIEL. People always do, don't they?

LUCY. I'm sorry?

GABRIEL. When have you ever heard someone say their sex life is bad? They never do. Because why would you stay in

a relationship with BAD sex? Unless there's something
wrong with your sex drive so, no, everyone has fucking
brilliant sex. Until they break up and THEN you get the real
story. How he rubbed himself up a cushion full of conkers
and she could only come if you sang the theme tune to The
Great Escape.

LUCY. But we do have good sex.

GABRIEL. Good for you, then. Do you fantasize?

LUCY. What?

GABRIEL. When you have your good sex, do you fantasize?
Sorry, it's just, if you have great sex and know you do then
you must be comfortable with it.

LUCY. I'm not gonna tell you that! It's none of your business.

GABRIEL. I think it's interesting. I think about two girls
together; spying from an opposite window while a woman
gets her kit off. And being tied up. Being king of the world
and all the women in the world all lying in a heap and they
want me so much they're foaming at the mouth like they've
got rabies, and all of them all over me, all licking and
writhing and moaning and hot and wet and boobs and they
all want me.

He smiles. Pleased with himself. And lights a cigarette.
LUCY *laughs. Then looks shy.*

LUCY. You think about your*self*?

GABRIEL. Why, you think I shouldn't?

He offers her the cigarette.

LUCY. I don't think about me.

She takes it.

GABRIEL. No?

LUCY. It would put me off.

GABRIEL. It would put you off?

LUCY. Yeah, I suppose so.

She's taken a puff and gives it back.

GABRIEL. Why?

LUCY. I dunno . . . I suppose I just don't find myself very
attractive.

GABRIEL. But you're the one having sex.

LUCY. I know. I try not to let that get in the way . . .

GABRIEL (*smiles*). So what do you think about?

LUCY. I don't know. Other things.

GABRIEL. What? Go on, I've told you mine.

LUCY. I don't know. Bodies. Abstractly I suppose. Just bits of bodies. And . . . I suppose . . . the man talking to the woman, saying things.

GABRIEL. Like what?

She shakes her head, embarrassed.

What, like, loving things? Dirty things?

LUCY. Like what he wants to do. What he's going to do. It's like, he wants her so much he's got to have her regardless of what she thinks, like he can't help himself, like he's powerless against his lust because she's so irresistible.

GABRIEL. He rapes her?

LUCY. It's not rape because she wants it too. She just . . . can't say so.

GABRIEL. Why not?

LUCY. Because . . . I don't know. It would be . . . It's just sexier if she doesn't admit she wants it and he does it anyway. She just wants him to want her so much he has to do it, rather than her admitting she wants it.

GABRIEL. Blimey. That's a bit complicated. I'm glad I'm a man.

LUCY. I used to think about doctors. But I suppose that's a bit of a cliché, really.

GABRIEL. So what else do you do? Toys?

LUCY. Joe brought some handcuffs from New York, official New York cop ones.

GABRIEL. Oh yeah?

LUCY. Yeah.

GABRIEL. Cool.

He waits for more but she says nothing.

Oh well, at least you have a good sex life.

She nods.

LUCY. He won't use them on me.

GABRIEL. He won't?

LUCY. No.

GABRIEL. Why not?

LUCY. I don't know. I do it to him, but he won't do it to me.

GABRIEL. Have you asked him?

LUCY. Yes. 'Course.

GABRIEL. But he won't?

LUCY. He just . . . I don't know. I think maybe he thinks it's criticism, like if I ask him to do something it means I'm not happy with what he was doing before.

GABRIEL. But you have to communicate in bed, else how do you know what the other person wants?

LUCY *half shrugs, then with difficulty –*

LUCY. Joe says you shouldn't have to say. It should be . . . wordless.

GABRIEL. Wordless?

LUCY. Yeah.

GABRIEL. So he doesn't talk to you at all?

LUCY. I think he thinks it's unprofessional.

She suddenly giggles irreverently. GABRIEL *smiles but is still pondering this.*

GABRIEL. What's the matter with him?

LUCY. I shouldn't have said anything, I'm being disloyal.

GABRIEL. We're just talking.

LUCY. Anyway, it's not a problem. Hardly a big deal.

GABRIEL. No.

LUCY. You won't say anything, will you? He'll be cross.

GABRIEL. 'Course not.

LUCY. Thanks.

GABRIEL. I'll be wordless.

LUCY (*smiles*). We're having dinner in tonight. We're finally gonna get a bit of time together. He's been so busy with work . . . and then out with my dad. We've hardly had any time to ourselves.

So what about you? Have you met any nice English girls yet?

GABRIEL. Uh . . . I dunno . . .

LUCY. Yeah?!

GABRIEL. Well . . . there is this one girl but . . . I don't know if she likes me.

LUCY. Bet she does.

GABRIEL. Well, she didn't spit at me. I took that as a good sign.

LUCY (*laughs*). I think she probably loves you then.

GABRIEL. She's got a boyfriend.

LUCY. Oh. Well, that's no good. Can't you kill him?

GABRIEL. Yeah, I dunno. She's not gonna be interested in me. She probably thinks I'm just some daggy bloke . . .

LUCY. 'Course she doesn't! She'll think you're a really good catch!

GABRIEL *looks at her and is about to respond when* JOE *appears, suited, home from work.*

JOE. Hey!

LUCY. Ooh hello!

JOE *nods at* GABRIEL, *but looks slightly guarded.*

JOE. Good to see you! How you doing?

He moves to kiss LUCY.

GABRIEL. Fine. Just giving Lucy a piece of a halo.

JOE. Why, has she been canonized?!

JOE *laughs.*

GABRIEL. She's working on it.

LUCY. Do you want some tea? I'll make some tea. Gabriel, do you want some?

GABRIEL. Er yeah. Sure. That'd be nice.

LUCY *goes inside.*

JOE. So what're you up to these days? I've been meaning to ask you, what is it you do usually?

GABRIEL. What do I *do*?

JOE. Yeah, you know. When you're not . . . travelling? What's your regular job?

Beat. Irritation.

GABRIEL. I'm a magician.

JOE. You're what?

GABRIEL. I do magic tricks.

JOE. Magic tricks?

GABRIEL. You know. Cards. Reading minds. Occasional alchemy . . .

JOE. What's 'alchemy'?

GABRIEL *looks at him. Stupid.*

GABRIEL. Turning base metal into gold.

A beat.

JOE. Base metal?!

GABRIEL. Uh huh.

JOE. You're shitting me. You can do that? You can't do that.

So go on then, show me. Show me this 'alchemy.'.

GABRIEL *looks at him for a long beat. Then he gives in with a smile.*

GABRIEL. And sometimes I work with computers.

JOE (*nodding*). *Computers* . . . (*He smiles, then laughs.*) Right . . . right . . . computers.

This seems to have answered some anxiety for JOE *and he visibly relaxes. Laughs again.*

You should come and help us out at the airport. BA has the shittiest anti-virus software I have ever seen. I'm trying to get them to change it, and if they do, we'll need some help. And it would pay a heap more than this labouring shit.

GABRIEL. Nice girls out there?

JOE. *Oh* yeah!

He laughs.

Everywhere you turn!

GABRIEL. Can't keep your eyes on the job, eh?

JOE. Well, you know, it's not easy . . . !

GABRIEL *smiles.*

GABRIEL. Nah. I'm alright. I think I'll stick with the 'labouring shit'.

JOE. Well, if you change your mind . . .

. . . but I guess . . . you won't be around that long, will you . . .

LUCY *comes out with tea and biscuits.*

LUCY. I even found some biscuits, which is a bit of a result!

GABRIEL *takes one but* JOE *declines, seems irritated with her.* LUCY *puts the tray down.*

JOE. All I have eaten today, is one apple and a banana.

LUCY. Well, that's not much.

She picks up a biscuit.

JOE. It's equal to my energy output. You *eat* more than you *do*, you gain weight.

LUCY *puts down her biscuit.* GABRIEL *notices.*

GABRIEL. You're having dinner in a bit though, aren't you?

JOE. Oh, I . . . er . . . told your dad I'd have a game with him.

LUCY. But! We said we'd have dinner!

JOE. You know Lucy, it's not all about you. He's your dad. And he called me, what was I supposed to do?

LUCY. I know, I / just –

JOE. And he's not well. That heart thing's really getting bad you know . . .

LUCY. I know. Ok. Fine.

GABRIEL. But I thought you'd cooked?

LUCY. Yeah but . . . it's probably horrible anyway. Just some weird fish. Thing. My cooking's crap. I nearly poisoned you the other day, didn't I . . . ?

JOE. I'll eat while I'm out.

LUCY (*laughs*). See what I mean?!

GABRIEL. Aren't you going with him?

LUCY. I . . . well, no I mean . . .

A beat.

JOE. Hey, you can come. I just didn't think you'd want to.

LUCY. I don't wanna . . . get in the way . . .

JOE. Come if you want.

She looks uncertain.

Come baby! It's all good!

He suddenly bear hugs her.

But don't spend half an hour getting changed or I'll have to hurt you.

A beat. He laughs.

LUCY. Right.

LUCY *picks up the ghetto blaster and takes it inside.* JOE *shakes his head.*

JOE. She always does that. You're just getting out and then she suddenly has to change her hair and find her lipstick and powder her fucking . . . teeth . . . whatever . . . I don't know . . . You know what women are like . . .

GABRIEL. Tell me.

JOE. Well, you know . . . all fucking . . .

But he's suddenly uncomfortable. As The Sex Pistols, 'Anarchy in the UK' starts to play from inside, he uses it as an excuse to change the subject.

What the hell *is* this?! What is she listening to? Are we in like, a time warp or something?!

Interval.

Scene Nine

SCARLET *enters, dishevelled from a night out where it looks like she's seen some action, eating a bag of chips.*

SCARLET. 1977. The year of punk and queenie's silver jubilee. A swelteringly hot day and there we are, 7b, stuck in an airless classroom while the teacher, who'd obviously rather be gang raped in a lay-by, mumbles into her moustache about the 'Facts of Life'.

I don't know why they bother. I mean, there's nothing in it that's any use, it's all, 'When a man loves a lady and is married to her and wants to make a baby, he puts lever A into sprocket B and out it pops.' They don't tell you anything useful. They don't tell you about the fact that you might also be able to *enjoy* it, or about diseases or about –

She laughs.

For instance . . .

There's a friend of mine who always seems to have this really amazing sex. She goes on and on about all these positions and multiple orgasms and how gagging for it she always is. But then one day, a few years ago, she was really freaked out because she thought she'd caught herpes. So she went to the doctor and said, 'Look, I've got this discharge and then there's this . . . *lump*.' So he has a look and he finds a bit of condom in there, one must have split or something – so he says, 'It's OK, it was just caused by that. You're fine.'

So she goes home, but then she rings me up in a state and says, 'Scarlet, I'm *sure* I've got herpes', so she goes back and she's got her legs up, and the doctor's having a look and he says, 'No, I really think you're fine,' and she says, 'But no! Look *there*! There's a lump!' and he's like, 'Where? Where? I can't see anything' And she's like *there*, you know, pointing. And he looks and he says, 'That's not a lump. That's your clitoris.'.

Anyway, so we're all sitting there, this bunch of ten-year-olds, sticky and sweating as we're copying pictures down from the board of how the penis works and this big hole we've apparently got inside us – *no* mention of the clitoris – and Lucy just keeps on asking these really stupid questions, I mean, like this is all *completely new* to her! She doesn't know! She *really* . . . doesn't know . . .

Afterwards I go off to get the bus, but I'm standing there like a lemon and of course, it hasn't come, so one of the other girls' mothers takes pity on me and phones my darling mother to say she has to come and get me because it really is awful to leave a ten-year-old standing there on the street.

So my darling mother turns up, in a foul mood, as usual, because she's had to interrupt her day for a brat and she hasn't even had time to eat so I can forget any idea about getting home in a hurry because she needs to stop to get some chips and I, of course, am not allowed to have any because I'm being punished for making her look stupid in front of another girl's mother. Again.

So she pulls into a car park, one of those big ones, and disappears over the road to the chip shop.

And I sit there, hating her and wishing she'd get run over, and then this man appears, right next to the car. I look at him, thinking he's going to get in the one beside us, but he doesn't. He just stands there, staring at me with this funny look in his eyes . . . and then he unzips his trousers and gets his thing out. And he starts to jerk it around, right close to the window where I'm sitting, his funny little face all red with sweat and his strange little eyes concentrating intently, trying to make out my nipples. It looks like hard work.

He jumps when I roll down the window. 'Do you need some help?' I ask. He doesn't understand. I wind the window back up and take my school skirt off, then my pants. I show him my fanny. His eyes start to bulge and his hand moves quicker on his thing. I stick my fingers inside myself and squirm around, like the women I've seen on the videos at home. I pretend I like it and make noises. His thing goes purple and looks like it might split, and then suddenly his come hoses all down the window with a splatting sound and starts to steam.

He looks at me almost reproachfully as he does his trousers up and then scuttles off. I put my skirt back on but not my pants. I leave them on the floor in the car as I get out, and very carefully start to draw pictures in the sperm, of houses that are safe and mothers who love their children.

I've only just got back in the car when my mother returns. I see her fury in the mirror as she catches sight of the mess on the window. I tell her some old bloke spat at us. She says I'm lying, she knows it was me. And she wipes it with her hand.

On the way home, I watch her eating her chips, the hand that wiped the window scooping into the bag, then up to her mouth, as she licks every last bit of salt off . . . and for once, for the first time in ages, I feel truly happy.

As SCARLET *turns away, she gets a text message and fishes for her mobile. As she reads it, lights come up revealing* LUCY, *a sheet wrapped round her, sitting at the table, waiting.* JOE *sleeps in the bedroom behind her.*

SCARLET *chucks away her chip packet, straightens her clothes, then heads to* LUCY.

LUCY *looks apologetic as she stands and hugs her.*

LUCY. Hi. Sorry. Thanks for coming. Were you awake?

SCARLET. Mm. Hungry. I don't suppose / you've . . .

LUCY. Help yourself.

SCARLET (*does so*). So what's up?

LUCY. Nothing. I just . . . couldn't sleep.

But she looks upset. As SCARLET *rummages,* JOE *now sits up in bed and addresses us.* LUCY *and* SCARLET *remain oblivious to him.*

JOE. You know what people do, when they meet me and Lucy?

SCARLET. Joe snoring, is he? Ergh, oh no, he's not trying to *cuddle* you, is he? I hate that, when you're trying to sleep and you've some man's bones tangled all over you and his breath in your / face and . . .

LUCY. No, he's . . . actually he doesn't do that. He keeps to his own side of the bed.

JOE. Lucy tells 'em she's an artist, and they're like –

JOE *puts on a super whiney American accent.*

'No, really?! Oh, that's so *interesting*!'.

LUCY. I just . . . can't sleep. I never can actually when there's a man in the bed. It seems rude somehow . . .

SCARLET. I think it's rude they don't just turn into a pizza when you've finished with them. I've never understood this whole 'sharing a bed' thing.

JOE. And then I say, 'And I'm a risk management consultant'. And they're like, 'Mn . . . ? So Lucy will you come and paint our portraits and aren't you just so wonderful?!'.

JOE (*laughs*). I dunno. It gets on my nerves, I guess.

SCARLET. I mean, you spend your entire childhood squeezed into some tiny single bed then you finally get to have a big one and it turns out you've gotta *share* it! So you end up on a tiny sliver, right out on the edge. And that's called 'happy'.

LUCY (*laughs*). Yeah, I know what you mean . . .

JOE. And she's all like, 'Hi, hi, hi, I'm so friendly . . . ' Everyone likes her. My whole family's like, 'Oh, Lucy's so nice . . . ' She asked me, 'Did they like me?' I told her, 'Yeah. Too much. Be *nastier*.'.

SCARLET. Sorry, anyway, you were saying?

JOE *now gets out of bed in his boxer shorts and moves towards us, to the centre of the stage, his clothes in his arms. Throughout his next speech, he gradually dresses for work – transforming from a boy in boxers, to a man in a suit – and during the scene* LUCY *almost seems to circle him.*

LUCY. Oh, I don't know . . . I just . . . or when I do sleep I've been having really horrible dreams. I was with this girl from school, do you remember the one who died?

SCARLET. Yeah, she was raped, wasn't she? Or was that the other one? God, isn't it awful when you can't remember who was raped. Anyway, yeah?

LUCY. Well, I was with her . . . and she had a Yukka plant, this big stalk with no leaves on it . . . and she was trying to tell me something but I couldn't hear her, so she got a knife and gouged a huge chunk out of the top of it, and it started spewing yellow sap, just everywhere, all over the table in front of me.

JOE. We went skiing last winter, whole family up in Vermont, and Lucy's like, 'Erughh, I can't do it. Will you show me?' Like a stupid little girl or something. Stupid. Why do girls do that?

He looks, as if in a mirror, as he does his tie.

LUCY. And I was looking down at the sap heading towards me and I knew, in the dream, that it was corrosive . . .

JOE. So I pushed her, I boarded right into her so she went flying. And she's like, 'Aw, Joe, why you gotta be so rough?' Hey, I'm a guy! We break things. That's what we do!

LUCY. . . . so I was trying to get out of the way but I couldn't move in time, so it slopped all over me and I remember thinking I have to get this off. I have to get this off . . .

JOE. I said to her, 'You know Lucy, if you ain't falling, you ain't learning.'.

LUCY. Because I knew that if I didn't . . . I would *die* . . .

Beat. SCARLET *still investigating food options.*

SCARLET. Mm. Cheese before bedtime, big no no.

JOE. It's all about risk – did I tell you that? What I do? I'm a Risk Management Consultant. It's all about risk baby!

He laughs infectiously as if parodying himself.

And you know, it's not about stopping planes falling outta the sky, this is 'em*ployee* risk.' *Oh* yeah! That's what it's about now, it's not about what you *make* anymore, it's about who you *got*, it's about getting the best people and keeping 'em, 'cause you're only as good as the people you got around you.

LUCY. I didn't have any cheese. I didn't eat at all actually. We went out with my dad.

SCARLET. Ah.

JOE. Do you know the biggest reason that's gonna make someone go off sick?

LUCY. Oh, it wasn't that bad.

JOE. Feeling like they're not valued.

LUCY. Well, he was drunk. They both were actually but . . .

JOE. Or that'll keep 'em out longer, if they get an injury and they feel like no-one's even calling to see how they're doing. You gotta make people feel *wanted*.

LUCY. He was having some argument with Joe about odds . . . he wanted me to go home and get some cards for him.

SCARLET. What, on your own?!

LUCY. Yeah . . . but he was just pissed. I thought about getting
angry but what's the point? He doesn't know how to
communicate with people . . . His own dad was such a
bully, I suppose he never had a chance to learn . . . Do you
think that? That maybe we get programmed and so beyond
a certain point it's too late to change or be anything else?

JOE. And when you investigate someone 'cause you think they
shouldn't be out, you gotta use *silence*. A cop told me that.
You create a *vacuum of silence* and it just sucks 'em in . . .

LUCY. Like those babies in Romanian orphanages who were
just left there, and no-one even touched them so later, when
they grew up, they couldn't love. There was a piece of their
brains that hadn't developed and now it was too late.

SCARLET. Mm. Maybe you're hungry? If you didn't eat?

She holds out her arms to kiss LUCY *goodbye.*

That'll stop you sleeping. You should make some porridge.
And the good thing about porridge is, it fills you up, every
last little space . . .

SCARLET *kisses her and leaves, stepping into bright
midday sunlight the other side of the stage.* JOE *remains in
his own early morning time frame, now almost dressed.*

JOE. It's the most powerful weapon you got, it makes 'em say
more than they want to, because they don't like silence, it
makes 'em unravel . . .

He steps on the end of LUCY*'s sheet and she unravels out
of it, coming to stand near* SCARLET *in a bra and skirt.*
LUCY *looks, as if into a mirror as she considers her body.*

LUCY. Scarlet, do you think I've put on weight?

SCARLET (*glancing up from the TV listings magazine she is
reading*). I don't know, have you?

JOE. I do it to Lucy sometimes, not that there's anything I
wanna *know*, I just want to see what she does. I give her this
look . . .

He demonstrates his silent look then laughs infectiously.

. . . and I just don't say anything, just sit there, and she gets
this look in her eyes, like she doesn't understand, so she
starts talking more like she's getting nervous, and she tries

to hold it together, but it's showing. So then she'll fish, like she needs me to say something nice, anything . . . but I don't. I just sit there.

And then she's trying not to cry. I watch it all come up and then she fights it back down again and swallows it. And then she smiles and says 'Ok, you're not in the mood to talk.'.

LUCY (*glancing behind her, as though hearing him*). I think Joe thinks I have.

JOE. It makes me wanna hit her.

SCARLET (*crossing to get* LUCY *a top*). Don't take any notice. He's an American. They choke on pretzels.

LUCY. Sometimes I think I catch him looking at me . . . this look in his eyes . . . like he hates me. Do you think that's stupid?

SCARLET. No. I don't know, Lucy, I mean, maybe it's not what you think.

She hands LUCY *the top.*

JOE *takes his laptop back and moves to a chair, as though at work, and turns it on.*

LUCY. What do you mean?

SCARLET. Well, you know, men are . . . they're not as *complicated* as us. He's probably just thinking about . . . what to watch on *TV* . . .

SCARLET *returns to the listings magazine and flicks on the TV.* LUCY *remains distracted as she paces slowly, unhappy, doing a circuit around* JOE.

LUCY. Mm.

JOE. I guess therapists use silence too. 'Cause they don't say much, do they? (*Laughs.*) Just expect you to tell all your secrets! Although I never got into that whole shrink thing. I went along a couple of times, but all they kept on wanting to talk about was the *past* . . . And it made me mad. You know, I don't wanna talk about the fucking past, I wanna talk about why things are going wrong *now*! Stupid assholes.

His computer booted up, he starts to type.

LUCY (*facing* SCARLET *again*). He got really annoyed with me last night. He got into this stupid conversation with a

waiter because he didn't know what 'mangey toots' were
and –

SCARLET. Mangey toots..?

LUCY. Yes, and so the waiter started laughing at him / and –

SCARLET (*cracking up*). Oh! No! 'Mange tout' . . . ?! Oh, he
didn't . . . !

LUCY. Well, he didn't *know*! And the waiter started acting like
it was the funniest thing he'd / ever –

SCARLET. It's hilarious!

LUCY. No it isn't, I / mean –

SCARLET. 'Mangey toots' . . .

LUCY. Well, would you know what an eggplant was? Or
zucchini?

SCARLET. Yes, they're both vegetables.

LUCY. Well, yes, OK, but you're a bad example because
you're into those things. And Joe isn't. And that's / OK –

SCARLET (*still laughing*). 'Mangey toots' . . . !

LUCY. Not the point! (*Beat.*) The point was he took it out on
me.

*SCARLET shrugs, not surprised. As LUCY moves back
'home' and starts clearing up the food mess on the table.
SCARLET picks up the sheet.*

*JOE laughs, remembering something. As he talks,
SCARLET starts to take her clothes off to wrap the sheet
around herself instead.*

JOE. You know, when I was a kid, this one time, I was playing
football, with the guys in my neighbourhood, and you
know, they were all bigger than me, like really big guys and
I was just a kid, around eight or so, and I was in there, all
keen, not gonna show 'em I was scared, and the ball hit me,
right there . . .

He points to his nose.

. . . and the pain was just . . . Uh! And I came home to my
mom, and I told her, and she's like . . .

He mimics her quilting, distracted.

'Oh Joe . . . just take two aspirins and go to bed . . . ' so all
weekend that was what I did, and then finally, on the third

day when I was like, *sick* with the pain, (*He laughs.*) she takes me to the doctors, and he's like, 'Yup. That's broken.'.

He laughs. Then seems disorientated, can't quite remember how he got onto this or what he was saying before. He shuts down his computer.

Lights for all of them change to evening.

SCARLET, *now wearing the sheet, is on the phone to* LUCY (*still cleaning*). SCARLET *glances at the TV.*

SCARLET. Oh God look at this! Don't you hate fucking television? I'm sick of all these Look-At-Me-I'm-A-Lawyer-And-Thin-And-A-Perfect-Mommy fucking stupid characters. If you're not going to show real women then FUCK OFF!!!! And none of them have got any body fat.

She flicks it off.

LUCY. Neither have you.

SCARLET. I'm working on it. Or I would be if I could find anything in this stupid house that wasn't anchovy paste! Who the hell has anchovy paste in their house?!

LUCY. Scarlet, where are you?

SCARLET. I don't know. Paris, I think.

LUCY. Paris!

SCARLET. Yeah. There's a bidet in the bathroom.

LUCY. Who are you with?

SCARLET (*peering off*). I'm not sure . . . Some man . . .

LUCY. Some man?! Well who?

SCARLET (*still peering*). My boss. It looks like . . .

LUCY. Well, what happened to Richard?

SCARLET. Richard handbag?

LUCY. No, Richard-who-gave-you-the-flat-for-free Richard. Richard you met in the bookshop.

SCARLET. Oh . . . I . . . He got pissy with me because I slept with someone else.

LUCY. Scarlet . . .

SCARLET. Lucy, he's married. Don't preach at me OK?

JOE (*standing with his laptop bag again*). When I was on my way over here, on the plane? There was this girl. She was sitting across the aisle to me, on the other side of the plane and every time one of us stood up or went to the bathroom, we clocked each other. And it made me feel mysterious . . .

He laughs.

LUCY. So who's Richard Handbag?

SCARLET. Oh, full of shit, looks good on your arm.

JOE. When I was standing by the carousel waiting for my bags, she stood right next to me . . . and there was / this moment.

LUCY. So you're seeing him now?

SCARLET. Who?

JOE. But I didn't speak . . . and neither did she . . .

LUCY. Richard Handbag.

JOE. . . . and then she took her bag and went.

SCARLET. No, look Lucy, I'm not seeing anyone alright? Well, I suppose I *am* still seeing Richard . . . sort of . . . Richard with the flat who I met in the bookshop. But, it's complicated. You know, I'm not like you. I can't do domestic bliss. And I don't want to talk about it. I'm hungry. I've just done one of those pound-pound-pound for hours jobbies without the aid of body fluids and now I need some porridge.

JOE. And I kept thinking about it, you know? What if? What if I *had* spoken to her . . . what if I'd followed her right out of that terminal and walked into a completely different / future . . .

LUCY (*looking out of her window*). I wish you liked Gabriel. I think you'd be good together.

Now LUCY *starts to undress again, but stays on the phone.*

JOE. Lucy says this thing, what is it? 'Character is action.'

LUCY. He's really nice.

SCARLET. Nnnn . . . he's not my type, Lucy.

JOE. Like, it's from one of those dumb film books. She wanted to be an actress once but she doesn't like being looked at. Or something. I dunno.

SCARLET. Anyway, there's something about him I don't trust . . .

LUCY. You say that about every man! You said it about Joe!

SCARLET. Yeah. Well, whatever . . . Anyway maybe I was right. You don't seem very happy . . .

JOE. But this book has these rules and this one she tells me like 'who you *are* is what will happen to you'.

LUCY. I think I just need to get a job.

JOE. I told her, 'That's fucking stupid. Like, what?! You can't *change*? It's all just fucking out there?' (*Shakes his head.*) Maybe for her. Not for me.

LUCY. I mean, I'm stuck here on my own all day, it's hardly surprising I've got nothing to say.

JOE. Oh no. I'm gonna invest in some clever stocks and make a pile of money.

LUCY. All I've got is what's going on in my head and that's not interesting, is it?

JOE. I'm gonna view American foreign policy with a cynical European eye. I'm gonna stop smoking, get fit, and get a good complexion.

He starts to undress for bed.

LUCY. God, I'm even bored of myself . . . no wonder Joe thinks I'm boring.

SCARLET. Does he say that?

LUCY. Who?

SCARLET. Joe.

LUCY. No. No. Joe doesn't say anything.

JOE. The first week I arrived in London, Lucy took me to see a play.

LUCY. Scarlet . . . ? I know this sounds silly, but I've got this idea into my head that I'm going to die.

JOE. By Mr William Shakespeare.

SCARLET. What do you mean? What of?

LUCY. I don't know. Nothing. I mean, maybe nothing. I don't know.

JOE (*he nods, knowingly*). 'Macbeth'.

SCARLET. You don't mean you're going to kill yourself?

LUCY. No. Well, I don't think so.

SCARLET. Well, what do you mean then?

LUCY. I don't know. I just have this idea that I'm going to die somehow. I told you it was stupid.

SCARLET. But you're not suicidal?

LUCY. No. I don't think so. I don't know. I don't really know how I feel. No, I mean, really, I don't. I don't know how people tell. I mean, I feel like I could cry . . . or I could be OK, I suppose. I don't know. Sometimes I feel like I'm acting, like I pretend to feel things just so I seem normal. So I seem like everybody else but really I'm just copying them, just copying what they do. I mean, it could be I'm depressed. Or maybe I'm quite happy. But I don't know.

She puts on her dressing gown. JOE, *oblivious to her, gets into bed.*

JOE. And I was thinking about that play, you know? Last night, before I went to sleep?

I was thinking what those witches would say to me, if I ran into 'em, underneath Waterloo Station or something.

LUCY. Sorry. I'm ranting. I'm talking rubbish. I should let you go.

SCARLET. Well take my advice and if you do do it, don't use pills because most people who take an overdose fail, and they just end up on dialysis with fucked-up livers for the rest of their lives.

LUCY. Is that true?

SCARLET. Yep. I reckon the best way to go would be to eat yourself to death. Just stuff and stuff until your stomach exploded! The only thing is, you'd have to make sure you ate all the food really, really quickly else your stomach would expand to make room and then you'd never actually get there, you'd just get really fat. Which would not be the point at all . . .

LUCY *laughs.*

Anyway . . . Well, promise me that if you get any stupid ideas into your head, you'll phone me.

LUCY. 'Course.

JOE. And I reckon the first one would say, 'Hail Joe, Prince of Risk Consulting!'.

SCARLET. Promise?

LUCY. Yeah. I promise.

JOE. And the second one would be, 'Hail Joe, King of Risk Services Division!'.

SCARLET (*glancing towards the bedroom*). Right then. I *suppose* I better go back in for Round Two. Don't you just hate it when you don't even know who's up your twot?

JOE. And then, the third one would be like, '*Hell* Joe! Why are you still in insurance?!'.

JOE *lies down in the bed.*

LUCY. Night, Scarlet.

SCARLET *looks at the sky and smiles.*

SCARLET. *Morning.*

JOE *closes his eyes.* SCARLET *and* LUCY *both hang up. Lights down on* SCARLET.

LUCY *enters the bedroom and watches* JOE, *sleeping, sprawled out. She sits on the edge, reaches out and touches him gently. He moves away in his sleep.*

Scene Ten.

Inside the snooker hall LUCY *plays on a Space Invaders game, but* JOE, *who is watching with* MICK (*both quite drunk*), *is getting annoyed.*

JOE. No! No! You're gonna die! You're gonna get . . . No, look see! You have to take out the bottom row! Why don't you just . . . Oh, give it to me!

He pushes her away and takes over the controls.

LUCY. Joe!

JOE. Well, you're gonna . . . Tsk, uh!

The space invader lands – game over. JOE *throws his hands in the air.*

LUCY. I was playing!

JOE. Yeah, like a crock of shit!

LUCY. It's a game!

MICK. Not to Joe. He takes these things very seriously . . .
Don't you, Joe?

JOE. No fucking point playing otherwise . . .

GABRIEL joins them.

MICK. Oh, hello then, deserter! (*To* LUCY *and* JOE.) You've
heard the news about this one then, have you? He's
abandoning me.

GABRIEL. Yeah, go on then, Mick, tell it all wrong.

MICK. He's leaving me for the church.

GABRIEL (*smiles, to* LUCY). They need someone to look
after the apartments . . .

MICK. Leaving me all alone. That's nice, isn't it?

GABRIEL. I'll still see you for a beer. I told you that.

MICK. I'll have to see if I'm available.

But he's joking and GABRIEL *smiles.*

GABRIEL. Alright then, you temperamental old git!

MICK. I think I hear my name being called! (*To* JOE.) Pwooh,
right then. Let's make it the best of three, shall we? Then
I'm off.

JOE. Sure!

LUCY. See you tomorrow, dad.

MICK and JOE *leave.* GABRIEL *sits beside* LUCY, *then
jumps up and briskly rubs her arms.*

GABRIEL. Hey little Lucy! You don't look very happy!

LUCY. I'm alright.

She smiles, he's infectious.

GABRIEL. You sure?

LUCY. Yeah.

I'm just a bit tired. I've been on the market all day. I'm on a
stall selling fluorescent stars that you stick on the ceiling . . .
and I don't seem to have time to do my artwork any more
so I end up staying up all night to do it . . .

GABRIEL. Well, that's no good!

She shrugs. It's OK. GABRIEL *looks awkward.*

I um . . . suppose I should . . . probably think about getting going quite soon . . .

LUCY. What, you mean going home?!

GABRIEL. Well . . . *going.* Going somewhere. I'll probably head back south for Christmas.

LUCY. We'll have to come and visit you.

GABRIEL (*smiles*). You won't.

LUCY. Yes I will.

GABRIEL. No you won't.

LUCY. Of course I will, why wouldn't I?

GABRIEL. Just . . . don't think you will. I dunno. People are funny. They say these things and then they . . . change their minds . . .

LUCY. You should have more confidence in yourself.

Beat. He looks at her curiously.

GABRIEL. Do you know what I like about you? I can't read you. I can read everyone but I can't read you.

LUCY. Well, I wouldn't try too hard, there's not a lot going on!

GABRIEL. Do you really not know what I'm trying to do here?

She just looks at him, blankly.

Spadework.

LUCY. Spadework?

GABRIEL (*nods*). Spadework.

Long beat. Then LUCY *suddenly giggles.*

LUCY. I don't know what that is!

GABRIEL. I'm *trying* to chat you up.

She laughs, nervously.

LUCY. Don't be silly.

GABRIEL. Lucy, you're awesome and you can't even see it! And you're stuck with that . . . McSuit over there! I want to bring you flowers every time I see you but I can't!

LUCY. God, it's a good job we *don't* go out together, you'd stress me out too much!

GABRIEL. He's playing around with someone at the airport, Lucy.

LUCY. No he's not.

GABRIEL. I saw him.

They were all over each other! He's not even trying to keep it a secret!

Well, aren't you angry?!

LUCY. We'll work through it.

GABRIEL. You'll wh / at . . . ?!

LUCY. We'll *work through it*! You can't just . . . run for cover every time it gets a bit hard! You have to understand / and try to . . .

GABRIEL. He's *sleeping with another woman*, Lucy! What's to understand?!

LUCY. He's done it before! He did it in New York! We worked through it! You have to *work* at relationships, Gabriel! Problems don't necessarily mean they're the wrong one, sometimes it means they're right! He just gets insecure because he thinks / I'm more . . .

GABRIEL (*realisation*). You think it's your fault.

LUCY. Of course I don't, I / just . . .

GABRIEL. You think he sleeps with someone else and somehow you're to blame.

LUCY. It's never black and white, Gabriel! It's / . . .

GABRIEL. You think it's because you're not enough. That there's something *bad* about you, something repulsive, like you've got to keep yourself away from people.

You think he's doing you a favour by even being with you in the first place, so you think you have to offer something else as well, and what that is, is being super nice and not making any demands and accepting any behaviour from him, no matter how unreasonable. And you're doing it all just to be loved, but all you're really doing is making him hate you for being such a victim.

Sorry that hurt didn't it? That really hurt . . .

LUCY. I thought you *liked* me!

GABRIEL. I do!

LUCY. What are you? Some kind of emotional terrorist?!

But he grabs her hand.

GABRIEL. I'm an angel. I'm the one who can give you what you want.

LUCY just stares at him. JOE comes over and clocks them both. He yanks at her skirt.

JOE. Hey! How's it going with the curtain skirt?

LUCY frowns.

Come on baby, aren't you getting up to dance on the bar?

LUCY. No. Of course I'm not.

JOE. Well, those girls over there are dancing on the bar! Don't you wanna join them?

LUCY. *No.*

JOE. I just thought it would be nice for you to do *something* other than sitting here like a sack of shit, for once.

GABRIEL (*stands*). I'm going. Have a good night.

JOE. Hey, but I was gonna give you a . . .(*game!*)

GABRIEL ignores him and leaves. JOE looks at LUCY.

What was that about?

Beat.

LUCY. He was telling me that I'm awesome and he thinks I should be with him.

Beat. Then JOE smiles.

JOE. Well, you know . . . one day.

LUCY. What does *that* mean? What does that mean – 'one day'?!

JOE. Well, you know. When our relationship's stronger, I'm just saying, it should be possible to sleep with other people.

Well, you're the one whose mum went off with someone else . . . !

LUCY. What's that got to do with it?!

JOE. I'm just saying. That's very interesting. That it was your *mum* who went off with someone else . . .

LUCY. She was unhappy! He made her feel like she had two heads!

JOE. She gave him a disease!

I mean, hell Lucy, what are we gonna do? Only ever sleep with each other for the rest of our lives? I'd be like Mike Tyson . . . end up chewing my own ear off!

Her face is on fire.

It was a joke, Lucy.

LUCY. No, it wasn't.

JOE. Yes it was, you know, funny? Remember when we used to do that? Laugh at things. Make jokes?

LUCY. That wasn't a joke.

JOE. No, right, 'course not. You're the expert. I forgot.

LUCY. Jokes are funny, Joe. They're funny things that make people laugh. Tell me what about that was funny?

JOE. Well, obviously fucking nothing because you don't have a sense of humour.

LUCY. I have a sense of humour! When things are funny, I laugh! But when things are cruel and spiteful . . . !

JOE. I'm not spiteful!

LUCY. Do you even find me attractive?

JOE. Of course I do.

LUCY. Do you?

JOE (*sighs*). You have to act sexy to *be* sexy, Lucy.

LUCY. And you have to feel sexy to act sexy.

JOE. It's stalemate then.

LUCY. But you find them attractive?

She indicates the girls dancing on the bar. JOE *looks.*

JOE. Yeah. Yeah I do. They laugh, they dance on the bar and they give me sexy little looks. I find them all attractive. It's just you I have a problem with.

LUCY. Why did you come here? Why did you even come?

JOE. Come on Lucy, this is . . .

LUCY. Why did you come? If you don't want to be with me, why didn't you just stay in New York and not put me through this?!

JOE. Alright!

You really want to know why I came?

To get away from the newspapers. To get away from every fucking day, opening the papers and seeing that some guy, who I went to school with, or who I played on the block with, has taken over some fucking corporation or is on the board of directors and is just going up, up, up!

To get away from their smug, fucking faces and their résumés and the constant running commentary from my folks . . . 'Oh Joe, did you see about Brad Haynes? His company just made the fortune 500. And Larry Stewart? He just floated on the stock exchange.'.

And you know something else? I was even pleased about nine eleven. Because at least it took some of them out of the running. At least it opened up a chance for me. At least some of them were fucking dead.

So that's why I came, Lucy. I came because I knew that then, when people asked after Joe, they'd be told, 'Oh he's doing great! He's living in London with this English girl, an artist, you know? Oh yeah, Joe's doing good.'.

LUCY. You've got till tomorrow to get out.

She turns and leaves.

Scene Eleven.

LUCY*'s living room.*

As she enters the phone starts to ring, and the answer-phone clicks on.

LUCY (*outgoing message*). Hi, Lucy and Joe can't take your call at the minute, so please leave a message.

Lights up on MICK *in a separate part of the stage, on the phone.*

MICK (*on the phone*). Alright, baby bear? This is daddy bear calling you from my tele-pho-ho-hone! Pick up the phone!

Pick up the phone if you're there? No? Not there? Not there, spud? Poor daddy all alone? Got no-one to play with, no-one to talk to, just sitting here, watching telly . . . Cor! Tell you what, some of these women are –

LUCY *picks up the phone.*

LUCY. Dad. It's me.

MICK. Oh you are there!

He chuckles, delighted. Slightly slurring, drunk.

I was just sitting here thinking I haven't spoken to Lucy for a while, I better give her a ring and see how she is . . .

LUCY. I saw you this evening! I saw you an hour ago!

MICK. Oh, was that only this evening?! Feels like longer than that . . .

He cackles with amusement.

LUCY. Look, dad I –

MICK. Just came home. Had me dinner. Must have gone for a kip. Nice bit of beef I had. Spuds and carrots . . . lovely . . .

LUCY. Look Dad, I'm –

MICK. Do you know Lucy, when you was little . . . I didn't love you. I tried to, but I couldn't. That's awful, innit? Awful . . .

LUCY (*upset*). Don't dad . . .

MICK. I wasn't interested in babies. What can I say? You know mate, it's the truth . . . didn't have any time for it . . .

LUCY. It doesn't matter, dad.

MICK. Yes it does. I'm a bad father, aren't I . . . ?

LUCY. No, you're not . . .

MICK. A bad father. I just . . . didn't get it. I never loved you enough . . . Couldn't hack it, mate . . .

I tell you what though, Scarlet! She had all the moves even then! Didn't she?! Even when she was ten years old! I couldn't be in the same room as her, she used to make me uncomfortable! Do you know that . . . ?

LUCY *is crying quietly.*

LUCY. I love you, dad.

MICK. I know, mate. And I love you too. I do, Lucy . . . I do mate . . . You're the only one who understands me..! I love you, Lucy . . .

He suddenly seems self-conscious.

Cor, what are we doing, here?

LUCY. What do you mean?

He starts to laugh.

MICK. I shouldn't be talking to you like that! Shouldn't be talking to me own daughter like that! Should I?! Should I! What the hell's going on here!?

He laughs.

Bloody hell, I'll be accused of . . . God knows what. This is out of order!

LUCY. No, it's not . . . !

MICK. Isn't it though!

LUCY. Dad . . . it's OK . . .

Beat.

MICK. Is it?

LUCY. *Yes*. Of course it is!

Beat.

MICK. I'm dying, Lucy.

LUCY. No, you're not . . .

MICK. This pain's so bad. I know it's a heart attack.

LUCY. What do you mean? Right now!?

MICK *suddenly draws in breath sharply.*

MICK (*in pain*). Uh! UH! I'm dying, Lucy . . .

LUCY. Dad, if you're winding me up, please don't 'cause . . .

MICK. *UH!* (*He clutches his chest again.*)

LUCY. Dad? *DAD*!? I'm calling an ambulance! I'm calling an ambulance now, OK? I'll see you at the hospital.

The lights change as LUCY *stands and put her coat on.*

I hurry through the evening fog to the hospital.

They say he's not there yet so I sit down to wait . . . five minutes. Ten. At the desk there's some confusion: they don't know whether the ambulance went or if there was no answer.

She stands, dialling on her mobile (we hear the bleeps and ringing).

I'm calling on his mobile, getting frantic: Nothing.

The landline rings and rings . . . I'm on the verge of starting screaming wh / en –

MICK (*off*). Lucy?

She crumples with relief.

LUCY. Dad? Are you alright? What's going on? Why aren't you here yet?

Her face changes to incredulity.

He tells me he's 'changed his mind'. He thinks his heart's OK. He's 'not coming to the hospital' . . .

Lights change as she leaves the hospital.

Outside the fog is clearing. Above my head a distant roar.

She looks up.

Tail-lights . . . I follow them to Gabriel's . . .

Lights up on GABRIEL *standing a little way behind her, bathed in yellow light from the stained glass window, as* LUCY *recalls.*

I find him and he's pleased to see me. Invites me in. Gives me wine. He kisses me and it tastes like love. Drowning in him, filling up. I'm melting . . . can't think, don't want to think, take me over, rub me out, no boundaries left. One flesh.

I feel him come inside me, that surge inside, flooding through my body and I know it's good.

I part like water. And let him in.

Scene Twelve.

SCARLET *sits at a reception desk on the phone, temping.*

SCARLET. Hello? Destiny Weekly? I don't know if he's . . . putting you through now.

Hello, Destiny Weekly?

LUCY *comes in as* SCARLET *puts the call through.*

LUCY. Hi. Are you free for lunch?

The phone rings again.

SCARLET. Two tics, Destiny Weekly? (*To* LUCY *as she puts it through.*) Uh, not sure. I was a bit late in.

LUCY (*smiles*). Who was he?

SCARLET. No-one. Just some guy. Don't start, OK? I'm not in the mood today . . .

LUCY. I wasn't going to. Scarlet, I . . .

SCARLET. Two tics. Destiny Weekly?

LUCY. I slept with Gabriel.

SCARLET*'s interested face.*

SCARLET. Just putting you through . . . (*Suddenly snaps into phone.*) No, I don't need to ask who's calling! I'm psychic, obviously. Read the fucking magazine.

LUCY. And I've told Joe to get out.

The phone is ringing again.

SCARLET. Well, thank God for that! He tried to get off with *me* four times!

SCARLET *picks the phone up, but doesn't take her eyes off* LUCY*'s gradually smiling face.*

Destiny Weekly? Yes. (*Beat.*) You're all going to die.

She pulls the phone out and grabs her bag.

Come on, let's go. (*To* LUCY*'s surprised face.*) Well, they're hardly gonna fire me! I'm shagging the boss . . .

Scene Thirteen.

A sense of outside. SCARLET *and* LUCY *walking, breezy. Perhaps autumn leaves.*

SCARLET. So, what happened?

LUCY. I don't know . . . I just . . . went bang I think. It felt such a relief just to let it all go . . .

SCARLET (*suggestive*). So . . . how was it . . . ? With Gabriel . . . ?!

LUCY. It was . . . *good*. I mean, I didn't come. I never do with just . . . you know . . . but it wasn't about that . . .

SCARLET (*disappointed / puzzled*). Oh . . . OK . . .

LUCY. He just . . . makes me smile. Makes me feel . . . safe. He makes me happy . . .

SCARLET. Oh. Ok, well, don't get too carried away with it though, will you?

LUCY. No. It's fine. He's leaving anyway. It's not about that. It's just . . . he's made me realise what's possible.

SCARLET. Mm.. I can't feel things like that. Maybe I should go and have my chakras opened or something . . . ? There's this man on the Holloway Road, maybe we could both go together and get a discount . . . ?!

LUCY. What's happened with Richard?

SCARLET. Oh.. I dumped him. He came round one day and I couldn't stop crying and when he asked me why I just said, 'Because there's no outside space.'.

Anyway, he was married.

Hey! That's another thing! At least now you won't be getting married! God, I hate weddings! The last one I went to, I was the only person there who'd slept with both the bride and the groom, although not at the same time and neither knew I'd fucked the other and the only other person who knew was the best man, who was getting more and more cunted by the minute and was in danger of including it in his speech.

LUCY *smiles*.

So what do you think Joe will do?

LUCY. I don't care. It's not about him any more, it's about me. I've realised how self destructive I've been being and I'm not going to do it again. The fog . . . has cleared.

SCARLET *smiles*.

SCARLET. The future's bright!

LUCY *smiles*.

LUCY. The future's *orange*.

Lights up on JOE *as they come down on* LUCY *and* SCARLET. *He stands awkward. Defiant.*

JOE. I went out that night and played pool like a God.

I don't care. I mean, what? Do I really want people to say, 'Oh yeah, Joe. He's the one with the dumpy, bitchy girlfriend'?

I hooked up with some guys from work and later we hit a strip joint. Absolutely hammered, on our knees. One of them hit some guy, I dunno, I joined in and there I am again, brawling with the boys back home, finally feeling part of something . . .

You know, Lucy used to say, the reason she loved me was 'cause I wasn't scared of dying. What I never told her was, it's because I'm scared of everything else . . .

JOE *turns away. Lights up on* SCARLET.

SCARLET. Sometimes when I lie in bed at night, my game is to go back in my mind to earlier times, retrace my steps to a place where other futures were still possible. Eight? Six? Where the damage hadn't been done and imagine a life like that.

But I can't do it. I always fall asleep before I get there, or else maybe I just can't remember that far.

I got an email from my father today, telling me about the latest sixteen-year-old African girl he's shagging, and saying I can no longer call him father because I'm too old. I have to call him 'Frank'. The words on the screen were dancing out at me and I felt like my head was going to explode with boiling wax or fat or something.

I needed to feel something else, so I phoned Richard, the only person I could think of who'd drop everything. He was on his way to the States but he told me to meet him at the airport hotel.

As SCARLET *arrives at the hotel we hear its sounds behind.*

All I wanted was a fuck, but he turns up, all moral high ground, thinking I'm after some kind of meaningful reconciliation. He tells me his wife has had cancer. She found out about our affair and the stress did it.

I tell him I'm not interested. We all have a story and that's hers. You live through it. You get on. Worse things happen.

Richard says I'm a cruel bitch. What's ever happened to me?

So I tell him.

How my dad had sex with me. How, when I was five, he drove me to Lucy's birthday party and instead of the chips he promised, it was his penis he stuck in my mouth, in a quiet spot along the way. How he told me I must never tell anyone, because I was the one who made him do it. And if I told anyone he'd leave. And how when I was eight he left anyway, without a word, in the night. And when I tried to tell my mother what he'd done she told me I was a spiteful little girl who made up stories just to hurt people. And that I must shut my mouth, and never, *never*, speak again.

But you know, it's really not that bad. You get over it. You cope. And it hasn't changed me. Not really. It hasn't made any difference to who I am.

One day I'll write a sitcom about him. I'll call it 'Northern Dad', and all 'e doz is drink beer an' fook underage girls. And 'e 'ates fookin' Southerners.

A strangled sound behind me and I turn to see Richard lying in a heap. Crying and blubbing with snot all down his face. And he's sobbing, 'No, no, how could they do that to you, Judy?!'

Howling like a dog. No, worse, like a *guinea pig*! Crying like I'm supposed to comfort *him*! Like it's *his* pain. And he tells me we can get through this. We'll do it together. Because he loves me.

I tell him that love's the last thing I want. That it's the worst thing anyone could do to me. Because it says, 'don't move.' It tells you to be perfect and never let them down. It puts you on a pedestal where you can't move left or right for fear of falling and you try so *hard*, to be real, to be pretty, to be good, to not do anything wrong, anything that will make them take that love away.

But no matter how hard you try, one day something you say or do, some curve of your body not right, a laugh too loud, or a mood too long and they glimpse that bitter blackness at your core, the sticky black darkness, gaping. Like famine. Like failure.

And the love goes out of their eyes.

She laughs.

It's like people who feel they have to stay awake on planes to keep them in the air. Because if they don't concentrate the plane will crash, so they can't relax, can't let their minds wander for even a nanosecond, because it's totally down to them to keep the plane up.

Same with love. It's too much strain. Easier just to let it crash.

She sighs.

I travel back on the underground . . . and when I come out it's foggy and all the streets look different.

I keep on going anyway . . . and I trip over a broken paving stone – I mean WHY DOESN'T SOMEBODY MEND THESE FUCKING THINGS BEFORE SOMEONE GETS *HURT*!!!

Finally lights come through the fog, lights that I seem to be heading towards, and as I put my hand on the buzzer, I see it's a block of flats.

There's a man at the door. Something familiar about him. He tells me he thought I was an ambulance. He's going to the hospital because there's something wrong with his heart. But first he needs a drink . . .

Lights up on MICK *as he pours two glasses of brandy.*

MICK. I don't know about you but I bloody need one.

SCARLET. Thank you.

MICK *hands one to* SCARLET.

MICK. Here mate. Tell you what, are you hungry?

He slides a huge plateful of chips over to her. SCARLET *stares at them.*

Thought you might like 'em. I can't eat. Made 'em but I can't eat. I'm too bloody worried about this hospital thing.

SCARLET, *slowly and mesmerically eating the chips.*

They alright, are they?

SCARLET. They're perfect. Thank you.

MICK. Lucy's coming with me. I don't think she was too happy about it.

SCARLET (*almost in a daze*). She won't mind.

MICK. She does. I get on her nerves. Always have done. Don't think she likes me much. I try, you know, but I don't know, always get it wrong, don't I?

SCARLET. No, you don't, Mick.

MICK. Yeah, I do. I know I do. Never been any good at any of it. Just some old fella . . .

SCARLET. Lucy won't mind, Mick.

MICK. Nah, she's a good kid. Not like she used to be, eh? Do you remember? Stropping round the place, chubby little ghost with all these screaming faces on her wall. She hated me. Do you remember? Round and white faced and she hated me.

SCARLET. She didn't hate you, Mick.

MICK. Yeah, she did.

Do you know, Lucy's the only thing I've done right. Do you know that? The only thing in my life I've done right. When she was born, I wrote a poem for her. I've never told another living soul that. I sat in the car park, couldn't stand hospitals even then, and I wrote her this poem. How tiny she was. And how I was scared to touch her in case I broke her.

But I felt a prat so I set fire to it in the car park.

He laughs.

I called it, 'Lucy In The Sky With Diamonds'.

SCARLET. I think that title might have gone, Mick.

MICK. Yeah, I know. I know, mate. Silly old fool. And now she's grown up and talented and the most important thing in my life. The *only* thing . . .

SCARLET *looks at him.*

SCARLET. I don't think there's anything wrong with your heart, Mick.

MICK. No?

SCARLET. No.

MICK (*nods*). Think I just drink too much, do you?

He holds her look for a long beat.

SCARLET. I think so.

MICK. Yeah. Yeah. Maybe you're right . . .

You know, if Lucy needed me, for *anything*, I'd be there. If she was ever in trouble, anyone ever hurt her, like a light, I would.

SCARLET. I know you would.

MICK. Anytime. Do you know, the day she was born they named black holes. Did you know that?

SCARLET. Mick?

MICK. I told her that. Creation and destruction in one. Just like women.

SCARLET *is very close. She touches his face gently. Strokes down it.* MICK *doesn't move.*

SCARLET. It's safe.

He's barely breathing. SCARLET *slowly moves towards him and kisses him. He looks frightened but he doesn't move. She kisses him again but he slightly pulls away . . .*

MICK (*gently, confused*). What are we . . . ?! What are we doing? You're almost like my daughter . . . !

SCARLET *looks very vulnerable.*

SCARLET. Please Mick . . .

He looks at her, frozen, then slowly, clumsily, moves back to her. A hug – which slowly relaxes. She kisses him again and this time, slowly and hesitantly, he starts to respond.

The phone rings. A moment, then MICK *picks it up, but he keeps his eyes on* SCARLET*'s face, as if she gives him calm.*

MICK. Lucy?

No, I'm . . . not coming. I've changed my mind. I think my heart's OK . . .

As MICK *hangs up and he and* SCARLET *continue kissing, (which will build up to slow and gentle sex with her straddling him on a chair, throughout the following scene) . . .*

. . . lights up on the other side of the stage, where LUCY *arrives at* GABRIEL*'s church. He opens the door, slightly wild eyed, bathed in yellow light from the stained glass window.*

LUCY. Hello! I . . .

GABRIEL. Lucy! What are you doing here?

LUCY. I just, I . . .

GABRIEL (*pulling her in*). Hey, it's good to see you!

He gives her a big hug then laughs.

I'm a bit off my head, actually. Just done an e. (*He bounces about.*) Do you want one?

LUCY. Er . . .

GABRIEL. Go on. You know it makes sense.

LUCY. Ok. Yeah, why not?

He leads her further inside and gives one to her. She takes it.

GABRIEL. Hey, so what's going on!

He hugs her again. Can't stop touching.

Oooh, it's so good to see you! So, what's happened? Did you dump the action man?

LUCY (*a bit dazed*). Yeah, I . . . suppose I did . . .

GABRIEL. You did?! Yay, yay!!

Dancing round her, grabbing her hands.

LUCY. I don't know. Is it me? Is it my fault things always turn out like this . . . ?

GABRIEL. Hey, no! No, Lucy, don't say that!

He grabs her breasts.

Oooh . . .

He lets go. Then, as if it never happened.

I can't bear that you think that about yourself.

He hugs her again. Starts to kiss her neck.

Here! Have some wine!

He hands her his pint glass of wine, but pulls it away at the last minute to wipe some of his own spit off it.

Oop, hang on! All my little germs in there!

She drinks some. He takes it out of her hands and starts to undo her top.

Oh, I have to do this. You don't mind, do you? Come on, let's dance . . .

With her top half off, he starts to dance with her, up close, putting his hand up her skirt. It's not clear if she's going along with it out of confusion, or need or sheer shock, but in spite of some hesitation, going along with it she is.

LUCY. Gabriel . . . ?

GABRIEL. I can't bear that you think that about yourself! Why do you put yourself down so much? You're great, fantastic, tremendous! What's got you so low? What's eating you?

He's all over her, almost got her clothes off.

Don't hide from me! Don't hide! None of us is perfect, Lucy! I'm not perfect either but that doesn't mean I can't have love! Does it? Everyone should have love . . . no matter what we think is wrong with us . . .

He pushes her onto a table.

I want to do everything to you . . .

LUCY. Have you . . . got a condom?

GABRIEL (*doesn't even falter*). I can't feel anything with one of them.

He's inside her.

Why you haven't got anything, have you?

He laughs.

LUCY. No . . .

GABRIEL (*still humping*). You came to my place! Told him to take a hike . . . Just a twat in a suit. I've wanted to do this since the first time I met you . . .

He's getting fast and furious. Turns her over, hardly sees her.

You're great, Lucy . . . you're amazing and you can't even see it. I'm gonna give you what you want . . .

Back to SCARLET *and* MICK, *the other side of the stage,* SCARLET *sits astride* MICK *as she quietly comes.*

SCARLET. For once he doesn't ask and for once the answer's 'yes'.

As SCARLET *strokes* MICK*'s face, and* GABRIEL *finishes his climax,* JOE *now enters the stage.*

JOE. I heard what happened to her, but I don't care.

I've got a new girlfriend already. I took her for a drink last night, then we walked back through the park. It would have been nice except for the sirens screaming past.

They must have gotten into my head 'cause when I went to sleep I dreamt a plane had crashed . . . or maybe it was just 'cause I was toasted . . .

Very quietly, we start to hear the sound of a plane above.

I've gotta cut down. I'm gonna give up smoking, invest in some stocks, and get a good complexion! Oh yeah! I'm on the way up, baby!

As GABRIEL *moves away from her,* LUCY *starts to itch. She scratches her arms and her legs, looking puzzled.* GABRIEL *leans in to kiss her goodbye as he reaches for his rucksack.*

GABRIEL. I've gotta fly.

As he leaves LUCY *itches more. Then more, frantically, tearing her skin to shreds.*

She starts to vomit as the sound of a plummeting plane grows. Itching and vomiting and holding her head.

The sound of a plane crashing deafeningly and then the sudden blare of music, Coldplay's 'Yellow', as LUCY *collapses.*

Scene Fourteen.

Sudden silence of a hospital ward.

LUCY *in a hospital bed, wearing a white gown, completely yellow jaundiced.*

A moment as we take this in, then lights up on SCARLET.

SCARLET. Lucy believes in omens. That the universe sends us signs of what's going to happen to us, what it's going to bring. Did it tell her this?

The doctor told her she'd contracted hepatitis B. They were sorry to say she'd caught it sexually. She phoned Gabriel, caught him just before he left. He said he knew he had it. He'd always known. He thought he'd mentioned it.

She considers this.

I don't know what to say to Lucy. Like I said, we've all got our own story . . . and I'm no good at comfort.

While I was there the doctors kept coming in, making the same bad joke . . . telling her she'd been Tangoed. But the funny thing was Lucy couldn't see it. When she looked at herself she couldn't see that she was yellow. She thought that was just the colour she'd always been.

She asked me to bring her in some clothes and make up. Something that would go with yellow . . .

As SCARLET *turns away,* LUCY *speaks surreally, as if reciting facts to keep herself sane.*

LUCY. On the 4th October 1968, John Wheeler named black holes. It was breakfast in Princeton and he'd just finished eating his egg. He gazed into the shell, at the yellow remains and it came to him: 'Black Holes'.

She smiles.

Do we choose our own destruction? Is there a point where we can't go back, where we're broken in a way that can't be mended and the only option is just to keep on going . . .

At first I was scared. What was happening to me? But then it started to make sense. *Had* he told me? Maybe he had . . . and maybe this is what I'd always wanted . . .

I met Joe in New York. I was out there for work. Or maybe running away. From something . . . I don't know. My dad was getting to me, I wanted to be as far away from him as possible.

I felt so free. Men looking at me like moths to a flame. And as Joe turned to me, something in his eyes . . . Something that said he wouldn't be easy, wouldn't be kind . . . That he'd make me as worthless as I feel.

And that look went right through me. Comforting. Familiar. Just like my father. That old look I wrap around me like the airline blanket on a night flight.

Lights up on SCARLET *in the hospital waiting room.* MICK *arrives with haunted eyes.*

SCARLET. Hello Mick.

MICK. How is she?

SCARLET pulls a face, not good. MICK nods. Beat.

Have they said what's wrong?

SCARLET. You better ask her.

MICK (*nods*). But she's . . . she'll . . . ?

SCARLET. I don't know.

She stands to leave.

MICK. Scarlet . . . ? I . . . we did, didn't we? You and me? We
did . . .

SCARLET. Yes Mick, we did.

MICK. But I'm . . . I mean, I didn't . . .

A beat, then SCARLET finishes the sentence that he can't.

SCARLET. . . . . catch anything. (*Smiles kindly.*) No Mick.

He also nods, finally acknowledging this.

MICK. Right.

Right.

He looks at her uncertainly . . .

So, should I . . . should I . . . *ring* you . . . ? Or something?

SCARLET. I'll see you soon, Mick.

MICK. Right . . . right.. well . . .

He indicates going in to see LUCY.

I better er . . .

SCARLET. Take *care*, Mick.

*He nods. And enters. Already sweating and loosening his
collar.*

MICK. Cor, I hate bloody hospitals . . .

LUCY (*smiles wanly*). Me too.

MICK. So, what's wrong then? Have they . . . ? What is it, like
. . . an infection or something? Is it?

A beat. LUCY looks away.

LUCY. Yes, dad.

MICK. An infection?

Beat.

LUCY. I think I must have just drunk too much.

MICK. Too much? Did ya? Yeah?! (*He laughs.*) That right?! Chip off the old block, you are!

So how long you going to be in here for then? Only I'm getting bored on me own . . . No, go on, only joking, you take as long as you need. Couple of hours even.

She smiles.

I er . . . heard you broke up with Joe . . .

Gotta be honest, I never really rated him. Sorry mate, but you know, I've gotta say it, n'I?

Never mind though. Better off on our own, aren't we? Me and you. Don't need no-one else.

He gets up to leave.

Hey! Had my heart checked out while I was here. Well, I thought I better. And do you know what?! There's nothing wrong! Not a dicky bird . . .

LUCY. That's good, dad. I'm pleased.

MICK. Yeah. Surprised me, I can tell you! I was certain, n'all! Funny old world, innit?

Right then. Well I'm gonna get back and have me dinner. Got a nice bit of fish tonight. Sweet n' sour sauce. Few spuds.

Tell you what, maybe I'll do dinner for you when you come out? That'd be a bit different wouldn't it? And now me cooker's fixed..

LUCY. That'd be nice, dad.

MICK (*smiles*). Yeah. Yeah . . .

LUCY. I'll see you later.

MICK *nods and leaves. Lights change.*

LUCY. Hospitals and airports are just the same. Arrivals, departures, and everyone else hanging around because something's gone wrong. At night, they turn the lights down, and you can almost see the sky . . .

Lights change – intensifying on LUCY.

The houseman came today. He said words like 'enzyme levels' and 'serious' . . . but I wasn't listening.

I was staring at his eyes. The bluest eyes I've ever seen. A perfect circle of aquamarine.

I imagine he's from Atlantis, a secret city beneath the sea . . . and as I stare into those eyes, I wish I could dive down into them, into that cool blue ocean which might just be big enough to wash me clean.

And suddenly I'm in a plane again. Gazing at the blue circle of sea beyond the porthole.

The sounds of a plane fade up as LUCY *gets out of bed.*

I get out of my seat. 30,000 feet. One last look behind me, then I open the hatch.

LUCY *opens an imaginary hatch and brilliant, bright light shines in on her, her hair billowing in the sudden rush of wind.*

The roar of the sky. The sea beneath me. Those blue, blue eyes . . .

I see myself plummeting towards this blue green planet. Because whether it's a plane, or a black hole, or a man who doesn't love me . . . the problem's always been gravity.

MALE VOICES (*echoing from scene one*). Jump, Lucy! Jump!

LUCY. Golden flames in the cabin behind me. I jump into the void.

As LUCY *steps out into the darkness, lights up on* SCARLET.

SCARLET. On 4th October 2002, Lucy died.

The funeral was ghastly. Mick didn't go, couldn't face it. Joe sent flowers. Afterwards I went to her house to sort out her things and while I was there, I found this magazine. A copy of the New Scientist, and on the front there was a picture of a person full of holes . . . and it said that black holes from the beginning of time could be inside any nucleus.

They could be inside *us*.

In the dark glass opposite there's a reflection of a woman. A woman who looks tired, like she hasn't stopped running for years. Like maybe she's been moving so fast so as not to see herself.

And behind her eyes, there's nothing.

She's nearly in tears . . .

I look at that reflection . . . and I find myself . . . *wanting.*

She laughs, trying to shrug off the emotion.

My dad's still in Africa, borrowing money off me. He's getting married again, to a woman half his age. My mum still won't believe me about him. Now she doesn't talk to me at all.

See what I'm like? I start on these stories and I can't finish them. I don't know what I'm saying anymore. I can't be around people . . . I've got nothing to say . . .

She leaves the things around her where they are and exits the stage.

Scene Fifteen

On board an aeroplane.

Sounds of boarding, the engine beginning to fire. GABRIEL *moves down the aisle looking at the seat numbers. He sings quietly to himself, The Verve 'The Drugs Don't Work'.*

GABRIEL (*singing*). 'All this talk of being lonely . . . It's getting me down my love . . . '

He finds the right seat, beside a WOMAN. *Twenty-something. Pretty. He moves into it, still singing.*

' . . . Like a cat in a bag . . . waiting to drown . . . this time I'm coming down . . . '.

The woman smiles at him. Can't resist.

WOMAN. It's 'old'.

GABRIEL. What is?

WOMAN. The words. It's 'Old.' Not 'lonely'. 'All this talk of getting *old.*'.

GABRIEL. Oh.

WOMAN. I like that. When people get the words wrong. It tells you something about them.

GABRIEL. Yeah? Like what?

WOMAN. I don't know. Maybe you're scared of being lonely? Maybe that's the worst thing you can imagine happening to you . . . being on your own . . .

A moment. Then he grins.

GABRIEL. Good job I've got you for company then.

WOMAN (*smiles, flirting*). Are you going to Bangkok?

GABRIEL. Yeah. Well, you know I'm just going. Going, going . . . Wherever . . .

WOMAN. Sounds a bit serious. Someone run you out of town?

GABRIEL. Well . . .

WOMAN. Girlfriend trouble?

GABRIEL. No, well, in a way, I suppose. There was this one girl. But it didn't work out.

She said I made her sick . . .

Blackout.

A Nick Hern Book

Airsick first published in Great Britain in 2003 as a paperback
original by Nick Hern Books, 14 Larden Road, London W3 7ST,
in association with the Bush Theatre, London, and the Drum
Theatre, Plymouth

Airsick copyright © 2003 by Emma Frost

Emma Frost has asserted her moral right to be identified
as the author of this work

Typeset by Country Setting, Kingsdown, Kent CT14 8ES
Printed and bound in Great Britain by Bookmarque, Croydon,
Surrey

A CIP catalogue record for this book is available from
the British Library

ISBN 1 85459 774 4